THE HANGING
OF
ARTHUR HODGE

A Caribbean Anti-Slavery
Milestone

64-ANDR

THE HANGING
OF
ARTHUR HODGE

*A Caribbean Anti-Slavery
Milestone*

John Andrew

To order additional copies of this book, contact:
Xlibris Corporation
1-888-7-XLIBRIS
www.Xlibris.com
Orders@Xlibris.com

With best
wishes —
To a good-friend Larry

John
Andrew

"In slavery days the black man's life count for nothing, but after the time of Hodge, a black man's life count the same as a white man."

Abednego
(An aged, life-long resident of Tortola,
reminiscing in the 1920s)

CONTENTS

LIST OF ILLUSTRATIONS

MAP

TO THE MEMORY OF MY PARENTS,
FRED W. AND FLORENCE E. ANDREW,
TO MY WIFE,
FLORETTA C. ANDREW,
AND TO OUR SONS,
SEAN T. AND BRETT T. ANDREW, AND THEIR
FAMILIES.

FOREWARD

My thanks for encouragement and assistance in this project are extended to my friends Jean Robinson and William S. Robinson, near
whose home on Great Camanoe in the British Virgin Islands I first
came upon a small coin stamped with the letter "H"; to the staffs of
the following libraries and research institutions who helped to iden-
tify that coin and assisted in developing the story that goes with it:
The National Library of Scotland, Edinburgh; the Archives of the
British Virgin Islands, Roadtown; The British Library; the Public
Record Office, London; the New York Public Library; the Library of
Congress; the library of the Association of the Bar of the City of New
York; the Boston Public Library; the Los Angeles Public Library; the
Huntington Library, San Marino; the Newberry Library, Chicago;
the Chicago Public Library; the Joseph Regenstein Library of the
University of Chicago; the Barbados Museum and Historical Society,
Bridgetown; the Institute of Jamaica, Kingston; the library of the
Genealogical Society of Utah, Salt Lake City; the General Libraries of
the University of Texas at Austin; the library of the New York Histori-
cal Society; the library of the Northwestern University School of Law;
the libraries of the American Numismatic Association, Colorado
Springs, and the American Numismatic Society, New York; and to
the Marquess of Exeter and Robert H. Solem.

I have endeavored to allow the actors in this drama to speak in
their own words as much as possible. Spelling and punctuation have
been changed and modernized where I have deemed it appropriate to do so.

Finally, my thanks go to my family—my wife Floretta, and our
sons Sean and Brett—for their long encouragement and support.

John Andrew

INTRODUCTION

The emancipation of the slaves in the British Empire—which preceded the American Civil War by almost thirty years—was the culmination of one of the lengthiest and most significant legislative battles of all time. Begun in 1787 with an attack by the twenty-eight year old William Wilberforce on the use of British ships in the slave trade, it was to end with the "utter" abolition of slavery by act of the British Parliament in 1833, as the aged Wilberforce lay dying.

The first act of the Parliamentary drama ended with the closing of the slave trade in 1808. Historians continue to debate whether the motives behind Parliament's decisions in 1806 and 1807 to abolish the slave trade and later, in 1833, to emancipate the slaves were humanitarian or economic. Surely they were both, but ultimately they were *political*. On a day, at a time, each Member present voted "yea" or "nay" and whether his primary motivation in casting his vote was humanitarian or economic, his action was political. "There is a story behind every bill," the legislative adage has it—and always it is a human story, with reaction to real events producing—in democratic societies—legislative reaction. So it was with this great reform in human behavior.

The promoters of slave trade abolition believed that it would lead to a gradual improvement in the condition of the West Indian slave population and a withering away of the institution of slavery without further parliamentary intervention. Only gradually did the realization dawn on them that radical surgery was required to remove the cancer of human bondage from the British body politic.

An important early step in that process of awakening was the reaction in Britain to the news, in 1811, of the trial and execution of a prominent West Indian planter, Arthur Hodge, a member of the Council of the Virgin Islands. Hodge, whose wealth and marriage had brought him high in English society, had been tried and hanged for the murder of one of his own slaves, Prosper—an event without parallel in the history of the British colonies in the Caribbean, where the master ruled the slave, but the law rarely ruled the master.

The charges against Arthur Hodge had been framed in the formal language of the law:

> "That Arthur Hodge. . . did command a certain negro man slave. . . to flog and whip the said slave Prosper and that in obedience to the command, and by the coercion of the said Arthur Hodge, the said slave. . . did then and there strike, flog, whip, bruise and lacerate the naked right and left buttock, and naked right and left thigh of the said negro man slave Prosper, for the space of one hour, in the presence of and by the command of the said Arthur Hodge. . . giving. . . divers mortal strokes, bruises, lacerations and hurts, of which. . . Prosper from the 2nd day of October. . . until the 15th day of October in the year [1807]. . . did languish, and languishing did live, on which day. . . the said slave called Prosper, of the said mortal strokes, bruises, lacerations and hurts so given. . . died."

The plea made on Hodge's behalf was simpler:

> *"That a negro, being property, it was no greater offense in law for his owner to kill him than it would be to kill his dog."* [2]

1

The Settlement of the Virgin Islands: "Good Night Governor"

The trial of Arthur Hodge for the murder of Prosper took place in Roadtown, on the island of Tortola, capital of the British Virgin Islands. From the court house one could look across Road Bay to towering Bellevue Mountain, on the slopes of which the Hodge plantation was located, and out to the blue waters of the Sir Francis Drake Channel and the islands beyond.

The British Virgin Islands lie in the Caribbean just to the east of the American islands of St. Thomas and St. John, which until 1917 formed part of the Danish West Indies. Further to the east and south are the British Leeward Islands, with which the Virgin Islands longed shared a common colonial governor. In 1811 all of the islands in the eastern Caribbean were ruled by the British, who had occupied the Danish, Dutch, French and Swedish colonies during the course of the previous decade and had conquered Trinidad, Spain's last possession in the eastern Caribbean, in 1797.

Tortola was described by a nineteenth century visitor as presenting "a highly interesting appearance, its mountains peaked and picturesque; and the plains below, clad with sugar cane." From a mountain peak one "obtained a view, at once, of almost all the islands of the Virgin group, with their satellites or cays. They are very numerous, and most rise very boldly from the sea. The scene was magnificent. There are no roads on this island for carriages— only rocky and precipitous mountain paths for journeys on horseback or foot. The wild plants are beautiful here. The great aloe, called the century plant, abounds and has a very picturesque appearance, and there are many prodigious plants of the cactus tribe. Pink, purple, red and yellow morning glories are seen creeping about in all directions.. . . The brown pelicans float about the coast in great numbers. Many of the hills are covered with luxuriant 'guinea grass' and afford excellent pasture for cattle, sheep and goats. The cows are sleek and beautiful and the milk excellent." [1]

In the early 1800s this tropical paradise was home to about 8,000 people. Seven thousand of them were slaves, employed in working the sugar plantations which had replaced the small cotton farms of the first settlers. About seven hundred "free people of colour" supported themselves as farmers, fishermen, merchants and domestics. A few hundred whites comprised the governing aristocracy of the island group.[2] They included the planters, their overseers, the factors and merchants who ran the economy and the island government with its multiplicity of offices and courts.

The Virgin Islands were the last British colony in the Caribbean to be settled.[3] They had been discovered by Columbus on his second voyage in 1493,[4] but it was not until 1648 that the first permanent settlement was established, when Dutch buccaneers built a fort on Tortola.[5] The Dutch were driven out by the English in 1672.[6] In 1685 the few English settlers were in turn driven off the island by a raiding party of Spaniards from Puerto Rico.[7] Only a few farmers, traders and smugglers continued to call the islands home until the 1720s when a number of settlers, fleeing years of drought on the island of Anguilla, obtained grants of land and brought their families, slaves and livestock to Tortola and Virgin Gorda (or Spanish Town, as it was sometimes called).[8]

These Caribbean pioneers lived virtually without government. William Mathew, who as Governor-General of the Leeward Islands was responsible for them, reported to his superiors in London that, "I know not what to do with the inhabitants of Anguilla, Spanish Town and Tortola. They live like so many bandits in open defiance of the laws of God and man." Indeed, "There's. . . a par-

The Virgin Islands from English and Danish Surveys, Thomas Jeffreys, 1775

ticular Lieutenant Governor to each of them, but if his cudgel happens to be a whit less than a sturdy subject's 'Good night, Governor.'"[9]

In 1734 Mathew, acting on his own authority, established a local government in the Virgin Islands consisting of an elected Assembly, an appointed Council and a Deputy Governor, selected by himself.[10] Moved no doubt by their knowledge of events during the bloody slave rebellion on the neighboring Danish island of St. John the year before,[11] the first action of the new legislators was the passage of a law bearing a lengthy but clear title: *An Act for punishing rebellious negroes, and such of them as desert their masters' services, and for the better encouragement of such of the Christian inhabitants or slaves, as shall apprehend, or take any such rebels as run away, so that they may be brought to justice.*[12]

Mathew approved the bill and sent it on to London for final approval.[13] There the government expressed its surprise and disapproval on learning that there was a legislature on Tortola and proposed that the Act be treated simply as "an agreement made by the inhabitants for their own safety, against their Negroes."[14] Once again the islands were without government.

A new element had been added to the community with the arrival of Quaker missionaries. The Quakers played an important role in the history of the islands for several decades and produced several notable individuals. Foremost among these was Dr. John Coakley Lettsom, the leading London physician of his day and founder of the Medical Society of London.[15] Dr. Lettsom's unexpected inheritance of large estates on his native islands in his old age would play a role in the chain of events leading to the trial of Arthur Hodge.

The lack of government plagued the settlers for many years until finally in 1774 a legislature on the pattern proposed by Mathew forty years before was established.[16] Years of debate concerning the settlement of land titles and debts were to follow.[17]

The first Chief Justice, George Suckling, arrived to establish his court in 1778.[18] He found the inhabitants in a "tumultuous

and lawless state . . . where life, liberty, and property are hourly
exposed to the insults and depredations of the lawless, the authority of His Majesty's Council, as conservators of the peace, defied
and ridiculed, for want of a proper prison; not one church erected
for the public exercise of religious worship; no court house erected
for the public administration of justice; the public debts unsatis-
fied, private credit sunk, and private property invaded." These conditions, he concluded, "added to the great scarcity and excessive dear-
ness of provisions, and every other necessary article of life, present a
shocking scene of anarchy, miserable indeed, and disgraceful to Government, not to be equaled in any other of His Majesty's dominions,
or perhaps in any civilized country of the world."[19]

Suckling returned to London in four months. He was succeeded by a local planter, Richard Hetherington, who was soon
removed for financial misconduct,[20] and then by James Robertson,
who had earned a death sentence from the victors for his services as
George III's Attorney General in Georgia during the American
Revolution. Robertson presided over the courts of the Virgin Islands—including the trial of Arthur Hodge—for thirty-five years,
until his death in 1818.[21]

Cotton had been the main cash crop of the early settlers. It
could be grown by family farmers with the help of only a few
slaves. Gradually cotton had been replaced by sugar as the principal export of the islands. The large capital investment required for
the production of sugar insured that only large planters would be
successful cultivators of sugar estates.[22] In 1784 Council President John Fahie wrote that, "It is here as it is elsewhere, the large fish
swallow up the small. The estates of the poor cotton planter which are
contiguous to sugar estates have been swallowed up by them."[23]

By 1787, when Arthur Hodge, then twenty-four, assumed—
as his father had before him—a seat on the colony's Council, the
economy and society of the islands had achieved the forms they
would retain for the next fifty years—the economy centered on
the large scale production of sugar and its by-product, rum, with
society dominated by the proprietors of the sugar estates.

2

The Planters: "Sons of Indolence"

Arthur Hodge and his peers, the sugar planters and their associates who were the social and political elite of the British Caribbean colonies in the early 1800s, were a highly privileged class.

In a colony as small as the Virgin Islands, this class included only a small number of individuals and a tiny percentage of the total population.

The 1812 census revealed only 405 white inhabitants in the Virgin Islands.[1] These included the merchants, attorneys-in-fact and agents who managed estates for absentee landlords, overseers and, of course, the resident planters and their families. Of complete families there could not have been very many—a visitor to the island in 1803 complained, perhaps with some exaggeration, that there were only thirteen white women, married or single, on Tortola.[2]

Under the circumstances, the number of white planters resident in the island must have been low, but they dominated the island, politically, economically and socially. Their life styles no doubt reflected their position in society. The author of *An Authentic History of the English West Indies*, published in London in 1811,[3] provides an enlightening survey of the daily routine of the master, like Arthur Hodge, of a Caribbean sugar estate. Characterizing him as a "son of indolence," he recounted his early rising and morning coffee ritual, involving "six or seven fine young slaves." Following coffee, the planter received his overseer and heard his reports on the work done the day before and the conduct of the slaves.

Flogging: "The Planter Looks on with calm Indifference as if Deaf to the piercing Shrieks that rend the air." (Frontispiece to The Authentic History of the English West Indies)

Should any of them have incurred the overseer's displeasure the planter ordered them punished. Punishments ranged from thirty-nine lashes "for a trifling failure of duty."

> "When crime claims greater punishment, the number of lashes are increased to one hundred, or as many more as caprice directs. The culprit, either man or woman, is tied to a tree, or [like Prosper] held down by four men, each holding an arm or leg; during this severe infliction, the planter looks on with calm indifference, as if deaf to the piercing shrieks which almost rend the air."[5]

Later in the morning the planter enjoyed a heavy and lengthy breakfast, described by one visitor to Tortola as "a meal fit for the Shah."[6] He then relaxed with a book, chess or billiards until retiring to his hammock for his mid-day nap. The planter would sleep until dinner, which generally began in the late afternoon. After dinner he would again hear reports from overseers and give orders for the next day. The evening was spent with cards, weak punch and sangaree, composed of Madeira wine, nutmeg, sugar and water. About ten or eleven o'clock he was undressed by his slaves and retired to rest. In the morning the routine began once more.[9]

The dress of the planter and his lady combined style and luxury with accommodations to the practicalities of tropical living.[11] The planter dressed in the style of England, but without "neckcloth or waistcoat." The ladies—described as "uncommonly fond of show"—likewise dressed after the manner of ladies in England, but "they dispense with whalebone, to which reason," Suckling, "attribute[d] the elasticity of their form."[12]

The Chief Justice also noted that "few ladies in the West Indies know better how to set out, and do, the honours of the table, than those of Tortola."[13] When it came to the "honours of the table" the West Indians generally made no concessions to the tropics. The planters slaughtered their own beef and mutton. Salt beef was imported from England and Ireland and all kinds of poultry and fish were to be found on the planters' tables. Most of their dishes were liberally laced with hot Cayenne pepper. Coffee was drunk in the morning; wine, rum punch and grog later in the day. Chocolate was a frequent supper drink. The "higher class of people" drank tea in the afternoon.[14]

Clement Caines, a lawyer and planter of St. Christopher, who had represented that island in the 1798 General Assembly of the Leeward Islands and whose *History of the General Council and General Assembly of the Leeward Islands* was published there in 1804,[15] wrote that, "An ostentatious profusion, a load of waste and victuals disgrace the table of every planter in the West Indies when he sees company."[16] The West Indians were, on the whole, proud of their reputation for hospitality. Caines saw it in a different light. Noting that the first settlers of the Leeward Islands had often been seamen who were, from necessity, in the habit of eating and drinking together, he railed,

> "The hospitality, which receives a stranger under its roof . . . cannot be too much applauded. . . . But the contemptible ostentation, which makes entertainments for people of fancied consequence, is not hospitality; though it ransack an island to please and gorge them. Nor is it hospitality to load a table with rare and costly viands, and to invite to it an hundred intemperate messmates, that they may practice gluttony and be guilty of intoxication. Nor is it hospitality for the master of a family to be restless and unhappy until he finds somebody, besides his wife and children, to eat with him a nicety, that happens to fall his way; as if the sweetest pledges of endearment, and the associate of his most exquisite pleasures were nobody. Nor does this unworthy father and unworthy husband partake of hospitality, when he neglects his most delicious connections to turn glutton and epicure abroad. To call these practices hospitality is an affront to virtue, and a profanation of language."[17]

The planter had little concern for the care of his estate, according to Caines, since, "When mention was made of the death of his slaves, he was ordering the turtle to be killed, examining which of his fat sheep was fattest, or which of his crammed turkies had throve most on its unnatural repletions."[18]

The drinking habits of his neighbors were also offensive. Examining the causes of vice—including drunkenness—in slaves, he wrote,

> "The habits of the country, its heat and thirst too, perhaps induce most people in the West Indies to drink too much. . ... But the bane of sobriety in the West Indies are a few men, who being themselves in the habit of daily company and regular intoxication, cannot bear that others should be either domestic or sober. . ... Two or three bottle men, as they are called, derive a title to be asked into the parties by frequently inviting large parties to houses of their own. And wherever they mix it is inconceivable to what degree they propagate drunkenness and profusion, a waste of time and a neglect of business. In sets to which they are admitted they always remain long enough to make all the company tipsy, and generally to intoxicate some most completely. Often the master becomes an accomplice. Although he may detest their practices, yet he cannot in his own house refuse a conformity to their inclinations. The consequence of a master's being intoxicated when he is surrounded with slaves may easily be conceived.[19]
>
> "That our house servants should acquire an attachment to liquor in consequence of their employment is not extraordinary. It would be extraordinary if they escaped the addiction, considering the scenes to which they are witnesses, and the temptations to which they are exposed, upon being introduced into our homes."[20]

As there were no roads on Tortola, the planters traveled over the island's "rocky and precipitous mountain paths" on horseback.[21] But they did not travel alone. The *Authentic History* observed that,

> "When a West India gentleman rides out on horseback he is usually followed by a negro, who runs after him with surprising swiftness; unwearied, he pursues, nor stops till he helps his master to alight. The negroes are uncommonly hardy, and almost invulnerable to fatigue; they can, with ease, support burdens that the strongest European would sink under."[22]

Caines saw this accouterment to travel by horseback in a different light. He recalled a former governor of the Leeward Islands whose Negro servant had ridden behind him on horseback. Complimented on his humanity, the governor,

> "told me that when he first came to the West Indies, he was fond of being attended by several of his finest negroes as running footmen, but that in a few years they almost all of them died of consumption."[23]

Caines further remarked that,

> "In this hot and overcoming climate I have observed that our fellow creatures supply the place of posts, pack horses, and carriage wagons, and the attendance at the greatest distance from their homes, which travelers meet with on their alighting at inns. If a note is to be sent a mile or two a negro runs with it, and must be back presently. Often of an afternoon, when a turtle has been unexpectedly caught, and a friend, for so we term those who eat and drink with us, and induce us to be guilty of excess in both respects, is to be invited to come the next day, and partake, away is sent the untireable negro to carry him a message or a letter for the important pur-

pose, although he lives eight or ten miles from the place where the turtle is to be eaten. When he attends too in consequence of the invitation a negro must run by the side of or follow his horse the entire distance, and must return with his master at night; sometimes, I am sorry to say, without tasting a scrap of the dinner, on which his master has been gorged. Ten miles too is no uncommon distance for a mistress to send one of her female servants before a ball, that she may borrow a new fashionable gown or tippet, or bring home a bandbox and its contents.

"I have known boys, who were mere children, called upon to run with their master seven or eight miles, or even a much greater distance of a morning and back again by dinner time. Nor was the object of this journey less contemptible, than the distance was merciless. The master, when he alighted, had no employment for his slave, but to hold his horse by the bridle, or lead him about after the ride, as he walked from house to house through the streets."[24]

Caines suggested that it would not be necessary to run a slave to town to hold the bridle of his master's horse if only livery stables were to be established in West Indian towns.[25]

In addition to "gluttony" and "drunkenness," the planter class found other ways to divert itself. "Dancing is the favorite amusement of the West Indians,"[26] the *Authentic History* records, also noting that, "They are remarkably fond of theatrical performances, . . . besides these they have assemblies and card parties, which in general are numerously attended, as they are great lovers of social intercourse."[27] It followed that "weddings in the West Indies are extremely magnificent, generally concluding with an elegant ball."[28]

Funerals were likewise major social events, "at which they drink burnt wine and eat the finest cakes." When a plantation owner died "every one of his negroes follows the mournful train, clad in mourning."[29]

The planters often had slave mistresses. According to Caines,

> "The female slaves in the planters' houses are all prostitutes;
> ready, willing, forward prostitutes; to the master, whether
> married or single, if he is addicted to women and variety.
> They are prostitutes also to his sons, when they grow up,
> before they grow up, as soon as infancy can be tempted to
> vice. They are prostitutes to every visitor, who chooses to
> send for them, and these prostitutes wait on his daugh-
> ters.[30]
> "The male domestics are likewise tainted by the infection of
> the atmosphere. The prevailing vices render them more de-
> based even than their vile estate; oblige them to execute the
> office of pimps for their masters, for his children, for his
> visitors. Or perhaps these instruments of sensuality become
> actors on the stage of lust, and purchase an instant of ecstasy
> at the risk of incurring the highest displeasure and severest
> penalties. For they are sometimes called on to supply their
> master's insufficiency in the arms of his too youthful, or
> insatiable, Dulcinea."[31]

A planter's child was suckled by a slave wetnurse and, while
very young, given a pair of slaves "so that by the time he comes of
age, (his slaves) sometimes increase to six or seven."[32]

> The little negroes follow their young master wherever he goes,
> like his shadow. At meal times they stand behind his chair,
> after which, they retire to eat the bits left on his plate, which
> are more or less, according to the child's generosity."[33]

The author of *Letters From The Virgin Islands*, who lived on
Tortola in the late 1820s, wrote that, "The slave progeny of a
household grow up almost foster-children with their little white
rulers."[34] Perhaps it was not always that idyllic. Referring to the
privileged status of the mulatto children of planters' slave mistresses, Caines observed:

> "To behold birds, and cats, and dogs, exposed to the thought-
> less or wanton barbarity of children is shocking. But to
> behold their fellow creatures, little wretches, scarce bigger
> than the urchin who vents on them his spite and fury,
> pulled by the hair, boxed and beat at the pleasure of a baby,
> excites a presentiment more horrid, than all that full grown
> tyranny can inflict."[35]

It is unlikely that the planters' legitimate children behaved with greater restraint.

The children of wealthy planters were not infrequently sent to school in England. Dr. Lettsom, for example, left the Virgin Islands at the age of six and did not return until he was twenty-three. Many, like him, probably never permanently returned to the islands.

The indulgence shown the planter as a child produced its inevitable results in the man. "Accustomed from early infancy to have their wishes anticipated, the slightest disappointment is considered insupportable, and too often produces that severity which is the great stain on their characters."[36] Summing up its description of a typical day in the life of a planter, the *Authentic History* concludes:

> "In this cheerless round of insipidity, he passes his life, un-
> marked by one act of benevolence; cruelty and selfishness
> are his characteristics; and while he riots in luxury, he disre-
> gards the welfare of those beings, who so largely contribute
> towards it."[37]

The women were no better:

> "Petulant and irritable, the females in this country are even
> more tyrannical than the men; for not totally divested of
> frivolity, they are troubled with many artificial wants. Impe-
> rious and overbearing, the West India woman knows not

self-command, and gives free indulgence to caprice. Gifted with strong mental powers, indolence prevents her from cultivating them. If she walks she complains of a fatigue, if she works she is oppressed with lassitude, and if she does neither she is still dissatisfied."[38]

Thomas Jefferson described his slaves as "capital"[39] and so they were. Thus it was only logical that the author of the *Authentic History* should write "As the English farmer prizes his stock, so does the West India planter his negroes, who are far more valuable."[40] The abolitionists forcibly argued that it was to the master's interest to treat his slaves well. Thomas Woolrich, a Roadtown merchant, testified before a committee of the British Parliament that it was his belief that their mistreatment resulted from "want of wisdom" on the part of the planters.[41] But it went deeper than that. He added that, "the masters of slaves become morose and cruel by being used to that kind of business, and that it considerably hurts the morals of the white people."[42]

Thus it was that, in the words of the *Authentic History*,

"the barbarity of planters exceeds even their avarice; and to their love of vengeance, they sacrifice interest. So irritable are their feelings, so ungovernable their passions, and so vindictive their tempers, that while punishing the slave, they forget he is their property. . .."[43]

And so it must have been with Arthur Hodge.

3

The Slaves: Africa and the Middle Passage—"We Were Not To Be Eaten"

In the early Nineteenth Century seven out of every eight inhabitants of the Virgin Islands were slaves.[1] Many of them had been brought to the islands from Africa. The rest were Creoles—natives of the West Indies whose parents or grandparents had made the same voyage and the same transition. To the planters they were "capital" but each was also an individual, with his or her own history, sorrows and fears, perhaps joys and even hopes.

All had been born weak and innocent, endowed with those inalienable rights, including life, liberty and the pursuit of happiness, of which Jefferson wrote.[2] Some, like five of the female slaves of Hodge's friend George Martin, lived to enjoy freedom and even inherit annuities from the estates of their former masters.[3] Others, like Hodge's slave Prosper, "languishing did live" until of the "mortal strokes, bruises, lacerations and hurts" of which they were victims they died.[4]

How were they brought into that situation? Thomas Woolrich, the Quaker merchant of Tortola, asked this question to many African slaves on the island. Among them was a waiting boy of his "who told him that he and his sister being catched together in the field, tending some corn," they were both carried away.[5] "Men slaves," he testified, "had told him they were surprised, and made prisoners by the enemy, in the night, in their own houses or village, others that they were prisoners of war."[6]

They were of many nations—Mandingoes from the west coast of Africa, Koromantyns from the Gold Coast, Eboes, Whydahs, peoples of the Congo and Angola.[7] Their European captors distinguished national traits in them. The Mandingoes were inclined, it was said, to theft.[8] The Koromantyns were distinguished by their courage;[9] the Eboes by the melancholy which frequently led them to suicide.[10]

Perhaps not atypical was Jumper Jem, who told his story to the author of *Letters From The Virgin Islands.* Born on the banks of what is now the Congo River, he was the son of "the least esteemed" of his father's three wives. The father, who had lost his noble status by marrying beneath his rank, acted as sub-agent to the native customs collector and—with his wives supplying most of the labor—raised pigs, sugar cane, pumpkins and tobacco. Thinking to improve his lot by procuring a firearm which would allow him to hunt for antelope and partridge, he resolved to sell Jumper, who was bow–legged and had one bad eye but was "a thick–set strong knave." Six days' travel brought the father, mother, another of the father's wives, and the son to the slave–trading post of Embomma, where the boy was traded for a fowling piece and some glass beads.

> "One trait," the son later remembered, "of human feeling was exhibited at the sale, and only one. The poor woman, his mother, on resigning her boy forever, burst into a passion of tears, dashed to the ground the necklace, her portion of the price of blood—and walked away sobbing to their canoe at the river–side."[11]

Bryan Edwards, a Jamaican planter and historian and member of the British House of Commons, related that his slave Cudjoe, who had been born in the Kingdom of the Ashantee (now part of Ghana), had been used by his older brother and guardian to satisfy the brother's obligation to the husband of a woman with whom he had been caught in adultery.[12]

During the last half of the Eighteenth Century well over 50,000 human beings were annually crossing the Atlantic in the holds of slave ships.[13] A perhaps typical shipload was that of the Spanish vessel *Venus* taken by *H.M.S. Barbadoes* and condemned in the Vice Admiralty Prize Court of Tortola in 1814. Abraham Mendes Belisario, a civil servant of many hats in the small world of the Virgin Islands—then wearing that of Marshal of the Court of Vice Admiralty—recorded in meticulous detail the names, ages, weights, and distinguishing marks of the cargo of the *Venus*. They numbered 303 when they arrived in the New World—27 boys and 29 girls under the age of fourteen; 198 men and 49 women fourteen and older. The oldest were men of thirty, the youngest a boy of seven. Many of the girls were ten, eleven and twelve. Most had African names— Wacrew, Omadaca, Ebayacha among the males; Ungwa, Yaza, Uzakko among the women and girls—but a scattering had acquired (or received from Belisario) European names, including Juan, Smith and Belisario. The tallest man was an even six feet. The second tallest, Ocurri, who was twenty years old, five feet eleven inches tall, with four spots on each cheek, hanged himself. Although apprenticed rather than enslaved, 107 of these young people were dead within a year.[14]

Olaudah Equiano, who had been a slave in the West Indies and America, having obtained his freedom, spent much of the rest of his life in Britain, where he published his autobiography in 1789.[15] In it he recounted his youth in Africa, his capture together with his sister, when he was eleven years old, and their final separation. Six or seven months after his capture he was brought to the coast, from which he was to share, with many million others over a period of 350 years, the horrors of the Middle Passage, the journey from Africa to America. Equiano was one of the few to make their voyage and later write of it. Thirty years after he had completed the Middle Passage his recollection of it was still vivid. He recalled his arrival on the coast, his first view of the slave ship and his terror when he was carried on board. Other memories included "the loathsomeness of the stench," being flogged for refusing to eat, "the galling of the chains, . . . the shrieks of the women and the groans of the dying."[16]

After weeks at sea, the voyage at last ended in the Caribbean, where the final step into slavery—the sale—took place. Equiano remembered the arrival in Barbados where merchants and planters came on board to examine the cargo, bringing with them "some old slaves from the land" who "told us that we were not to be eaten, but to work. . ... This report eased us much."

He described the sale, which occurred a few days after the landing.

> "On a signal given (as the beat of a drum), the buyers rush at once into the yard where the slaves are confined, and make choice of that parcel they like best. The noise and clamor with which this is attended, and the eagerness visible in the countenances of the buyers, serve not a little to increase the apprehensions of terrified Africans, who may well be supposed to consider them as the ministers of that destruction to which they think themselves devoted. In this manner, without scruple, are relations and friends separated, most of them never to see each other again. I remember, in the vessel in which I was brought over, in the men's apartment, there were several brothers, who, in the sale, were sold in different lots; and it was very moving on this occasion, to see and hear their cries at parting."[17]

Like Olaudah Equiano, the author of the *Authentic History* commented on the deliberate separation of families and friends when the newly arrived slaves were sold. "Such is the spirit of cruelty that exists in the bosom of some planters," he wrote, "That I have known them, after purchasing two negroes who proved to be husband and wife, send them to different plantations."[18]

Equiano concluded his description of the Middle Passage demanding

> "O, ye nominal Christians! might not an African ask you — Learned you this from your God, who says unto you, Do unto all men as you would men should do to you?"[19]

Some observers described a recovery period during which a new slave was "kept clean, instructed and well fed, without working, for six weeks, during which from living skeletons they become plump and fat, with a beautiful clean skin."[20] But Woolrich testified that, "After the arrival of African slaves in Tortola, they are generally kept a few days before they are put to field labour. (I) never knew any who were not put to labour a week after they were purchased."[21]

4

The Slaves: Life in the West Indies:
"A Predominant Melancholy"

However they came there the slaves, once arrived, were subject to the customs and laws of the Virgin Islands. These had been codified in the Virgin Islands Slave Act of 1783—a document of forty–nine clauses which clearly reveals the concerns and fears of its drafters.[1]

They got right to the point: the first clause provided that slaves accused of committing serious crimes were to be tried before three Justices of the Peace and, if found guilty, to be sentenced to death or any other punishment they deemed appropriate, with immediate execution to follow.[2]

Slaves who ran away to hiding places amid Tortola's mountains or on the offshore cays must have been a serious concern to the planters. More than a quarter of the Slave Act is devoted to runaways. Individual runaways could be punished by death for a single absence of three months or more or for being gone for more than six months in a two year period.[3] If a gang of ten or more from a single plantation was gone for ten days or more the ring-leader was to be executed.[4] Slaves condemned to death for running away were to be appraised before execution and the owner compensated for his loss,[5] but—to discourage frequent prosecutions —the compensation was not to exceed £50 for a male or £45 for a female slave.[6] Free Negro, Indian, Mustee and Mulatto men could be ordered by any Justice of the Peace to join the hunt for runaway slaves.[7] Those pursuing them were empowered to break into the slave houses on any plantation to search.[8] Anyone killing a runaway who had been out for more than three months was to receive a reward of £3—for a runaway brought in alive the reward was £6.[9] Slaves found aiding others to escape were to receive from fifty to one hundred stripes.[10] Whites harboring runaways were subject to fines increasing from £20 currency to £100 currency, plus other monetary penalties.[11]

The planters lived with the fear of violence from their slaves. The sale or bartering of weapons to slaves was forbidden and slaves were not permitted to carry "fire–arms, cutlasses, swords, pikes or lances, or other hurtful weapons" off their owners' plantations without a pass or under the "direction of a white person then present."[12] A slave found with weapons was to "receive thirty–nine stripes on his bare back, or such other punishment as the Justice in his Discretion shall be pleased to inflict."[13] The Act also provided

> "that if any Slave or Slaves shall impudently strike, or oppose any white person, any Justice upon complaint and proof made, shall order a Constable to cause such Slave or Slaves to be publickly whipped at his discretion, and if resistance [is offered], such offending Slave or Slaves shall have their nose slit, or any member cut off, or be punished with death at the discretion of the Justice, always excepting that such Slave or Slaves do not the same by his or her Owner or Employer's order, or in defense of his or her person or goods."[14]

The fear of poisoning was endemic among the white planters in the Caribbean. The Virgin Islanders specifically provided in their act that any slave found guilty of having attempted poisoning should suffer death, with his or her owner being compensated out of the Treasury.[15]

The Act closely regulated many aspects of slave life. Slaves were not to leave their plantations without passes except on Sundays and holidays when they were allowed to visit the market between sunrise and eight o'clock at night.[16] Slaves were to have two days holiday after Christmas, but no more.[17] Owners giving them more time off at Christmas, or allowing them to avoid work on Saturday mornings, were themselves subject to fines.[18]

The fear of insurrection prompted the enactment of a clause forbidding slaves "to unseasonably beat Drums, blow Horns, or use any loud or alarming Instruments."[19] Gatherings of slaves from different plantations were forbidden.[20] Masters were required to search their Negro houses at least once every three months for runaways, weapons, drums and contraband.[21]

Noting that slaves had "endeavoured to imitate White persons in pompous and expensive funerals," the legislature decreed that slaves were only to be buried in plain board coffins and not to be buried after sunset.[22] Slaves wearing scarfs at funerals were liable to receive up to fifty stripes.[23]

The economic life of the slaves was also closely regulated. They were not to own any slaves themselves, nor any horses or cattle, although goats and hogs were permitted to them.[24] The raising of cotton by slaves was strictly prohibited, the legislature believing it to be a cause of the decline of the small plantation owners.[25] It was forbidden to purchase a wide variety of goods—including sugar, cotton, rum, wine, clothing and household items—from slaves.[26] Peddlers, whether slave or free, were forbidden to hawk their wares except in the Negro Market on the customary market days.[27]

Prior to the passage of the Slave Act slaves had been permitted to hire themselves out as porters, paying their owners for their time. This custom was found to have resulted in many runaways passing themselves off as slaves for hire and in an increase in the number of robberies. To correct these abuses the act required the registration of porters and the issuance to them of metal badges (not unlike modern taxi medallions) which they were to wear while on duty.[28] The number of badges to be issued, whether to slaves or free Negroes, was limited and the rates which they could charge were set forth in the statute.[29]

Gambling also claimed the attention of the legislators, who

found that "many mischiefs and inconveniences have arisen and so daily happen from the maintaining and encouraging of sundry Idle, loose and disorderly Mustees, Mutlattos and Negroes, as well free as Slaves, in their dishonest and dissolute Course of Gaming to the circumventing, deceiving, cousening and debauching of many of the younger and better sort. . .." It also found that "this Evil . . . also tends to promote frequent Robberies and Thefts, to support the practitioners under their losses at Play. . .." To correct these abuses it was decreed that any white involved in "Cards, dice, Billiards, Tables, Skittles, Shovelboard, Quoits, Nine–pinns or . . . Cock–fighting" with a colored person be fined from fifty to two hundred pounds.[30] A free person of color so involved was subject to fine and from thirty–nine to fifty stripes.[31] Slaves found gaming were subject to "whipping, Pillory or Imprisonment."[32]

It should be noted that the evidence of slaves was not admitted against white persons in the courts, although it could be admitted against other slaves.[33]

The "Slave" Act contained several clauses which specifically regulated the activities and rights of free Negroes and other persons of color. All were required to choose a white "patron or protector . . . who may render an account and answer for the Tenor of . . . their Conduct and Lives. . .."[34] Free persons of color, like slaves, were to be whipped if they should "presume to strike any white person (Servant or otherwise)."[35] Those who repeated the offense were subject to the death penalty.[36] Whites striking free persons of color were to be punished at the discretion of the Justices.[37] The free colored were not permitted to own more than eight acres of land and those owning more than fifteen slaves were subjected to special taxes.[38] These provisions suggest that some among the free colored population had begun to acquire substantial amounts of property.

Marriage between slaves and free persons was prohibited.[39]

The future of the newly arrived slave depended, in large measure, on the nature of the work to which he or she was assigned.[40] The planters competed with each other in the number of their attendants[41] and every "great house" establishment required the non-agricultural work of a number of household slaves. These included cooks, seamstresses, laundresses and the men who waited on table. They were generally dressed as European servants and ate the same food as their owners, although the size of their portions was carefully controlled.[42] In addition slaves were responsible for the care of the planters' children[43] and did the work of coopers, carpenters, masons, millwrights and smiths.[44]

The bulk of the slave population, however, was composed of field hands who worked the sugar and cotton plantations. The newly arrived African who was destined for field labor first went through a period of "seasoning" in which he learned the daily routine of the plantation.[45] This seasoning, Woolrich testified, was the leading cause of death among the newly arrived slaves, with one-third or more dying during the first year.[46]

The field slave usually began his labor at dawn. At eight or nine o'clock he or she was allowed a twenty minute break for breakfast. Work was then resumed until about noon, when a two hour break was taken for "dinner" and the picking of grass to feed the plantations's horses and cattle. Field labor then continued until half an hour before sunset.[47] Sundays, and sometimes Saturday afternoons, were free.[48]

The work of the field slaves included hoeing, planting, weeding the crops, and carrying manure to the fields in baskets borne upon their heads.[49] During the five to seven months a year in which the sugar was ripening the slaves might find themselves working in the fields until an hour or two after dark to supply cane for the mills. The slaves who worked at the mills and in the boiling house commenced their labor as early as an hour or two before sunrise and continued for two or three hours after dark.[50] Their labor was not as physically hard as that of the field slaves but was tedious and accompanied by dangers of its own. Indeed, it was said that, "So very dangerous is the work of those negroes who attend the rollers that should one of their fingers be caught between them, which frequently happens through inadvertence, the whole arm is instantly shattered to pieces, if not part of the body; a hatchet is generally kept ready to chop off the limb, before the working of the mill can be stopped."[51]

At the end of the day West Indian field hands recommenced the picking of grass. This task was perhaps the hardest and most deeply resented of the slave's responsibilities[52]. The grass was picked blade by blade, root by root, while darkness fell, until each slave had gathered his bundle and returned to the works where the bundles were inspected before being fed to the horses and cattle. Those whose bundles were too small suffered what Caines described as "trifling" punishment. Coming at the end of the long day, the grass gathering frequently found the slaves so tired that failure to complete their bundles was the most frequent reason for slaves running away.[53] Caines declared that the anxiety to collect a satisfactory amount of grass often compelled the slaves to work through the noon–time break without eating.[54]

The women among the field slaves did the same work as the men. The *Authentic History* records that

> "the owner of a plantation, insatiate for gain, always sends a man and woman to work together, by which contrivance, the work of two men is generally performed; as the poor negro will double his diligence, to lessen the sufferings of his unfortunate companion, who is, perhaps, his wife, mother, or sister, far advanced in pregnancy, a state that exempts them not from the severest hardships."[55]

The daily diet of the slave included salt fish and beans or yams with a rare portion of pickled pork.[56] On Saturday afternoons, Sundays and, when possible, during rest periods, the fortunate slave might raise some vegetables and chickens to supplement his diet.[57]

The slave's daily portion of food was not sufficient to sustain the hard labor which was his lot.[58] In Tortola, according to Woolrich, there was never a certain supply of provisions for the slaves.[59] During the twenty years he was on the island he saw the slaves' provision grounds steadily diminish in size while the food imported for them did not increase.[60] He had known slaves to die for want of food.[61]

Caines observed that "on many estates in the Leeward Islands the Negroes are fed indifferently and inadequately."[62] During crop time, when the slaves were permitted to chew sugar cane in the fields and drink cane juice at the mill, their normal provisions were reduced by a quarter or a third.[63] Yet although their work was hardest at this season they appeared to be healthier than at other times because of the nutritive value of the sugar.[64]

The slaves lived in small square huts, which they built with poles, and thatched at the tops and sides with palm leaves or other available materials; a few had cabins of boards.[66] "These houses are built very near each other, like a village closely huddled together,"[67] and were "so small . . . that when the door and windows are shut it is a perfect stove. . .."[68] Most slaves slept on the ground in the middle of their huts with no bedding but warmed by a small fire. Some were able to obtain a mat or board to use as a bed.[69]

The clothing of the men consisted of a pair of trousers and of the women of a petticoat given them once a year by their owners.[70]

The *Authentic History* notes that

> "In their persons they are very clean, males and females
> usually bathing twice a day; to supply the place of a comb,
> they use clay, which being dried on the head, and washed
> off with soap and water, frees them from vermin."[71]

They cleaned their teeth and sweetened their breath with sprigs of the orange tree.[72]

Slaves were not allowed to marry.[73] Bryan Edwards argued in the House of Commons that they had misery enough without adding matrimony to their lot.[74] But many of those who could formed lasting unions. One of the *Letters From the Virgin Islands* mentions an aged couple who had lived together on the same es-

tate for almost fifty years.[75] Edwards himself, while speaking of
"an almost promiscuous intercourse with the other sex,"[76] remarked
of the slaves that

> "When age indeed begins to mitigate the ardour, and lessen
> the fickleness of youth, many of them form attachments,
> which strengthened by habit, and endeared by the con-
> sciousness of mutual imbecility, produce a union for life. It
> is not uncommon to behold a venerable couple of this stamp,
> who, tottering under the load of years, contribute to each
> other's comfort, with a cheerful assiduity which is at once
> amiable and affecting."[77]

Despite occasional examples of great longevity, the life expect-
ancy of the average slave was short.[78] Caines attributed this to the
"excess of their toil and the scantiness of their food."[79] The *Authentic History* blamed their early deaths on "the want of attention
to the condition of the female field negroes, and to the over exer-
tion of the men for their relief."[80] "Death," it declared, "is the
only friend the negro knows."[81]

The birth rate among the slaves appears to have been unnatu-
rally low. Caines attributed this to three causes: "premature as well
as indiscriminate venery, scantiness of food, and excess of labour,"
with the last the most important cause.[82] He considered the slaves
to be "tutors in iniquity" to their children, blaming, in part, the
closeness of their quarters for this condition.[83] He noted that young
girls often contracted venereal diseases which left them sterile for
life.[84] To support his view that "excessive and indiscriminate venery" reduced the likelihood of conception he quoted a Negro prov-
erb: "Grass never grows in the common path."[85]

With reference to field labor, he observed that "Toil, unrea-
sonably protracted, and then renewed without sufficient intervals
of rest, diminishes the wish of sexual intercourse, and with its
frequency its effect too."[86] He remarked that

"negro women, who have been barren in the field, become prolific when taken into the house, where their rest and food, particularly the former, have been increased, notwithstanding their usual–perhaps an augmented–addiction to venery. The same observation never, I believe, applied to women who were removed into the field from the house. They never breed there, if they were barren before the removal."[87]

Abortion and miscarriage were common.[88] Although Caines considered the practice of abortion among the "rich and great" in England "as unaccountable as it is vicious,"[89] he was not surprised that the slave mother "destroys her children while in the womb," for if slave parents "fleeced of their rights and destitute of hope" have a child, "his inheritance is poverty and degradation, perhaps wretchedness. He is born a slave."[90] Caines attributed miscarriages primarily to the carrying of heavy burdens to market and the frequent quarrels and fights which occurred there.[91]

Infant mortality was, as might be expected, very high. Caines noted that a large number of children died with convulsions during the first nine days of life.[92] He assigned several reasons for these deaths. First, he noted that the slave huts were close and usually very warm, but so small as to be subject to rapid cooling if a door should be opened at night, subjecting the infants to unexpected chills.[93] He also noted that the slaves had picked up dangerous English habits–including that of administering "a nauseous potion of castor oil" as soon as the baby was born–and, despite the heat, wrapping infants in swaddling cloths, which were frequently "soaked through and through with urine."[94]

As soon as the mother was able to do so she returned to field labor, her child being entrusted to the care of an old woman, who would bring it to the field for suckling. During this period, out of swaddling clothes and spending a large portion of the day out of doors, slave children enjoyed an "astonishing superiority" over the whites in health.[95] But upon weaning "they become weaker and sicklier than the white children, sink below them in growth, (and) are assailed by disorders peculiar to themselves. These disorders hurry many of their victims to an infant grave, and intail upon many more infirmities and decrepitude which endure as long as they live."[96] These conditions followed weaning, Caines believed, because of malnutrition resulting from the master's failure to increase the child's rations at the time he was deprived of his mother's milk.[97] Nor was it unknown for "bad mothers" to consume themselves the bulk of the meager ration provided for their children. The young child was "left and neglected in the negro houses, where he has to contend with filth, insects and diseases, in addition to famine."[98]

Caines concluded:

> "To this multiplied mortality among the infant negroes it is owing, that every succeeding generation of slaves in the West Indies is less numerous than the one which went before it; that the whole race would become extinct, and every island in which they are labourers would become an uninhabited desert, if a perpetual drain on the devoted population of Africa did not fill up the unnatural void, which servitude and its consequences create."[99]

Elsewhere he declared of the field slaves that "the excess of their toil and the scantiness of their food spread among them a premature mortality, and renders fresh drains upon Africa necessary to fill up the deadly and unnatural void."[100]

"Fresh drains" were, of course, made upon Africa and the planters were increasingly driven into debt to pay for new supplies of their "capitol." But, as might be expected, and as Thomas Woolrich testified before Parliament, "The slaves of those who are much in debt are generally more severely and worse treated, than slaves of such as are in easy circumstances."[101] This cycle of deprivation, death and debt increasingly fed upon itself and the peoples of west Africa.

Even the life of a slave was not without its occasional pleasant moments. Sundays, holidays—including the two days after Christmas—and sometimes Saturday afternoons were their own.[102] Then they could cultivate their small garden plots, sell their vegetables and chickens in the market, go to church, or relax amidst their friends and families. The nights were theirs also—most often for exhausted rest but on Saturdays, at least, for music or worship.

Though they played at games of their own—the *Authentic History* mentions awarce, played by pitching marbles or nuts[103]— their principal recreations were music and dancing.[104] "Every Saturday night," the *History* records, "the slaves who are well treated close the week with a dance—besides which they have a grand ball once a quarter."[105]

Edwards appears not to have cared for their music; the author of the *Authentic History* enjoyed it. Edwards wrote of the goombay as "a rustic drum" and remarked that "from such instruments nothing like a regular tune can be expected, nor is it attempted." "In general," he complained, "they prefer a loud and long–continued noise to the finest harmony, and frequently consume the whole night *in beating on a board with a stick.*"[106] This board was the qua–qua, "a hard sounding board, raised on one side like a boot jack, on which they beat time as on a drum, with two pieces of iron or two bones," whose inventors the author of the *Authentic History* termed "ingenious."[107] The maligned goombay he described as "the great creole–drum—a hollow tree covered at one end with a sheep–skin, on which they sit astride, beating time with the palms of their hands, producing the effect of the bass viol to the qua–qua board."[108] Their other instruments included the "banja" or "merriweng," played like a guitar, and "dundo" or tabor drum and a reed flute.[109]

Caines wrote that the slaves often sang as they worked, producing "a very animated and pleasing effect," and daring, in their songs, to remind a master "of promised and ungiven holidays, additional allowance, or change in the kind of their food, when long sameness has rendered variety desirable."[110] Edwards observed that

"their tunes, in general, are characteristic of their national manners; those of the Eboes being soft and languishing, of the
Koromantyns, heroic and martial. At the same time, there is
observable, in most of them, a predominant melancholy, which,
to a man of feeling, is sometimes very affecting."[111]

At their "merry meetings and midnight festivals"[112] the slaves
always danced in couples, "the men figuring and footing, while the
women turn round like a top—their petticoats expanding like a
hoop."[113]   Edwards found their dances "in the highest degree licen-
tious and wanton"[114] and the songs which accompanied them for the
most part "fraught with obscene ribaldry."[115] Another who found
their dances "filthy" and "lascivious" was Dr. Thomas Coke, the founder
and historian of the Methodist missions in the West Indies.[116]

Each of the slaves had left all of his or her material belongings in
Africa; but each of them arrived in the West Indies with a spiritual
heritage. Their religious beliefs were little understood and less appre-
ciated by their Christian captors. But then a devotion to their own
Christian religion was not one of the outstanding characteristics of
the West Indian slave–owning class.[117]

Thomas Woolrich, in twenty years, never knew an African who
did not acknowledge a Supreme Being.[118] Many of those brought to
America from the northern part of the west African coast were, as
Edwards and Caines noted, Mohammedans, some of whom could
read and write Arabic.[119]   But most worshipped other gods. Olaudah
Equiano remembered that in his homeland

"the natives believe that there is one Creator of all things,
and that he lives in the sun. . ... They believe he governs
events, especially our deaths or captivity. . .."[120]

He remembered that

"we never polluted the name of the object of our adoration;
on the contrary, it was always mentioned with the greatest

reverence; and we were totally unacquainted with swearing, and all those terms of abuse and reproach which find their way so readily and copiously into the language of more civilized people."[121]

The feature of African religion which most attracted the imperfect attention of the whites was the practice of Obeah, which the English considered a form of witchcraft or sorcery. According to Edwards, the priests of Obi were always natives of Africa. "The Negroes in general," he wrote,

> "whether Africans or Creoles, revere, consult and fear them; to these oracles they resort, and with the most implicit faith, upon all occasions, whether for the cure of disorders, the obtaining revenge for injuries or insults, the conciliating of favour, the discovery and punishment of the thief or the adulterer, and the prediction of future events. . .. A veil of mystery is studiously thrown over their incantations, to which the midnight hours are allotted, and every precaution is taken to conceal them from the knowledge and discovery of the White people."[125]

The Obeahmen were reputed to have the power of life and death over those who incurred their wrath or that of those among their adherents who turned to them for the righting of wrongs. One old woman in Jamaica was reputed to have killed over a hundred of her fellow slaves through the practice of Obeah during a period of fifteen years. Finally revealed to her owner by her daughter–in–law, who believed that she had put Obi upon her, the old woman was given to a party of Spaniards and taken to Cuba.[127]

Clement Caines wrote of a sect of the Obeah, known as Confu, whose votaries awakened from drunken stupor to tell of beatific visions which they had enjoyed while asleep and asked philosophically, "[W]hat religion is without its sectaries, or the arrogant pretension of being the true church?"[128] Referring to the period before the arrival of the Methodist missionaries, Dr. Coke, who believed that he belonged to the true church, wrote of the Negroes of the Virgin Islands that

> "Among other branches of iniquity to which they were addicted, there was one they termed the *Camson*, a practice which at once gratified their sensual appetites, and indulged their native superstitions. The Camson was a filthy, lascivious dance, originally imported from Africa, in which every lustful inclination was indulged to excess,"

including "acts of the most ferocious brutality" directed by the dead with whom they communicated.[130] The magistrates tried to suppress the practice of Camson but its adherents clung to it "with an eagerness that was proportioned to the strictness of the prohibition."[131]

The slaves believed in an afterlife in which they would return to Africa and enjoy the happiness denied them in the present.[132] Their cosmos did not, however, include a place of eternal punishment.[133]

When a slave died his body was brought to the door of his owner by his relatives, who loudly "declare the unwillingness of the deceased to leave his master."[134] Burial was accompanied by heroic dancing and singing, since death was "a deliverance which, while it frees them from bondage, restores them to the society of their dearest, long–lost and lamented relatives in Africa."[135] After burial it was customary to bring offerings of food to the grave. One writer noted that the belief that the dead received these offerings was encouraged by the fact that they were frequently stolen by runaway slaves.[136]

Although persecuted, discouraged and—from the end of the Eighteenth Century on—subject to Christian prosetylization, many of the Africans clung tenaciously to the religious beliefs of their childhoods. Edwards wrote of Flora Gale, who died in Jamaica in 1792 at the age of 120. He found it remarkable that she "always refused to be baptised, assigning for reason her desire to have a grand Negro dance at her funeral, according to the custom of Africa; a ceremony never allowed in Jamaica at the burial of such as have been christened."[137] Referring to the failure of the Jamaican authorities to stamp out the practice of Obeah, Edwards quoted the conclusion of a correspondent from Jamaica "that either this sect, like others in the world, has flourished under prosecution; or that fresh supplies are annually introduced from the African seminaries."[138]

In the Virgin Islands the influence of African religion had seriously declined by the 1820s.[139] Christianity—and particularly the new Methodist Society—had, in the meantime, come to play an important role in the islands. There was neither chapel nor minister when the first Methodist missionaries arrived in Tortola in 1789.[140] Their missionary efforts were at first highly successful and by 1796 they claimed a membership of more than 3,000 in a total population of about 10,000—with "love feasts" being celebrated not only on Tortola but on Spanish Town, Anageda, Great Camanoe, Peter's and Jost van Dyke as well.[141] Almost all of the early converts were blacks or mulattos. This no doubt was a reason for the "warm persecution" which the missionaries endured during their first years in the islands.[142]

This persecution was followed by a period of such acceptance that in the mid–1790s the Methodist missionary Turner was asked to lead a force of Christian Negroes who were armed to prevent a French raid on the island.[143]

By the end of the decade the number of blacks and mulattos in the society had begun to decline, although the relatively small number of white members continued to increase. This decline resulted in part from the practice of the Methodists, like that of the Quakers forty years earlier, of expelling members who were guilty of "improper conduct."[144] It was accelerated following the suppression of a revolt in which Methodist slaves were involved in 1799. The missionaries were required to appear before the Assembly to defend their role. Finding that they were not implicated, the Assembly passed a resolution forbidding slaves to assemble for worship unless a missionary was present. It was also decreed that slaves were no longer to be received into the society without written permission from their owners.[145] In the coming years slaves were to be punished in Tortola solely for attending Methodist services.[146]

Another reason for the loss of slave members was emigration. In 1796 the British had conquered the Dutch colony of Demerara, now part of Guyana, east of Venezuela on the north coast of South America, and British planters looked to the new conquest for increased opportunities for profit. In 1799 "great numbers" of slaves, including Methodists, were removed from Tortola to Demerara.[147] A similar movement was to occur after the conquest of Trinidad from Spain.[148]

The missionaries were proud of the submissiveness which the slaves learned from their Gospel. Despite 1799, they would later claim "that no slave, under the care of the missionaries, has ever been detected in a single conspiracy."[149] Missionary Brownell reported from Tortola that Christian slaves so much enjoyed the trust of their masters that they not only served as drivers, boilers and watchmen but had actually supplied the place of white overseers.[150]

Whether Christianity brought other benefits to the slaves was open to debate. Clement Caines complained of a slave who stole to be able to have something for the collection plate. "It is," he declared, "to be wished that these holy pastors would abolish these collections, and also the sacrifices of roast fowls and boiled legs of pork, which the pious negroes piously offer up to their spiritual visitors, and which their spiritual visitors most carnally devour."[151] The missionaries themselves told, with approval, of two female slaves who had each contributed a small coin, known as a "black dog," to an elderly obeahman before their conversion and afterwards robbed him of a like sum to celebrate their adhesion to Christianity.[152]

Caines, with a true Eighteenth Century spirit, considered the conversion of the Africans from Obeah to Christianity the exchange of "mysteries for absurdity."[153] Observing that "these poor wretches . . . will still drink and steal while talking of their Redeemer and Heavenly Master" and that "moral duties . . . are neglected, while religious ones are performed," he blamed the missionaries who "told them of the necessity of faith, the operation of grace, the nature of the holy spirit, with the pleasures of heaven and the pains of hell" but who neglected to preach "common honesty and mere truth" for their failures and predicted that "As long as this mode of instruction is persevered in, our negroes will regularly go to church and say prayers on Sundays, and they will regularly steal, game, fornicate, and get drunk the rest of the week; nay, on Sundays too, as soon as service is over."[154] Switching to a footnote, he went on, wondering as to the effect on "the poor negroes" of the doctrine of the Trinity and "the cohabitation of the Holy Spirit with the mother of God."

There was much to be said for the Koromantyn god Accompong, noted by Edwards as:

> "[T]he God of the heavens, . . . the creator of all things; a Deity of infinite goodness; to whom . . . they never offer sacrifices, thinking it sufficient to adore him with praises and thanksgiving."[123]

5

The Slaves: Death in the West Indies: "Mutilated Limbs and Broken Hearts"

The slaves lived under a regime of which physical coercion, often imposed with great brutality, was the very essence. "Compassion," the *Authentic History* recorded, "is a stranger to the planter's bosom."[1]

Moral judgments—conscience—depend upon time and place and circumstance. But additionally they depend upon a determination of a proper course of behavior, unique to each person, the correctness of which may be judged against a universal standard, dimly perceived, based upon the collective experience and judgment of humanity. We are neither slaves nor slave–owners. Our world has moved on from theirs. We cannot judge them as they judged themselves. But we can consider their self–judgments and compare their actions with our perceptions of universal standards of human behavior.

Clement Caines, a lawyer and a planter, in describing the cruelties of Negro slavery as he saw it in the British Leeward Islands near the close of the Eighteenth Century, noted that West Indian slavery was not unique in his world. He compared it with the military and naval establishments of Europe, in which flogging was a way of life and slavery was "imposed under other names," and observed that,

> "The vassals of Hungary and Poland are still wretched, the
> boors of Russia still humbled in the dust. The Turkish slave
> is still condemned to the bowstring; and the African still
> decapitated by the sanguinary skill of a practiced despot."[2]

The abuses of West Indian slavery, he believed, arose from the *absolute* control of master over slave. In that, he compared it with the "systematic and inexorable (slavery) practiced by the despots of Europe" and concluded that

> "although the absolute power of the planter could never be reproached with the cool and reflecting tyranny of Europe; yet it has its whips and scourges, its grated dungeons, it bolts and its bars, its chains and its fetters. It maimed and mutilated too, as powerful cruelty has elsewhere done. Nay, it celebrated its *Autos de fes*, and rivalled the fiery zeal of religion, by burning men for rebellion on earth, as the ministers of the God of mercy have burnt their fellow creatures for rebellion against heaven."[3]

Already subjected to extreme brutality during the process of enslavement and his or her transportation to the New World, the newly arrived slave often faced a lifetime of continued cruelty. In many islands (though not often, according to Woolrich, in Tortola)[4] the first ordeal to be faced was that of branding, an operation performed, according to Edwards, with a silver branding iron which forever marked the slave as the property of his first owner.[5] Thus the slaves who were first sold to the Codrington plantation in Barbados, owned, by devise, by the Society for the Propagation of the Gospel, forever bore upon their breasts the word SOCIETY or the initials S.P.G.,[6] while those sold to other estates bore the initials of their owners.

Edwards, who had never been branded, believed the pain to be momentary.[7] He may have been correct—yet one suspects that a burn which left a life–long scar involved more than momentary pain. His understanding of branding no doubt helps to define the border between those who experience and those who report. So it is with much of the literature of West Indian slavery. To begin to understand the feelings of those personally involved one must not only read, one must not only try to picture in the mind's eye, one must try to feel—the lash on the back; the lash in the hand. The lash, whether held in the hand or received on the back, touched the soul as well as the body. "Mutilated limbs and broken hearts," Governor Hugh Elliot was to write in a report on the Hodge trial, "have withdrawn thousands of bondsmen from a life of servitude."[8]

*   *   *

The lash, or cart whip, the symbol of planter authority, was commonly made of rope–like flax or hemp and sometimes of thongs of cattle hide, twisted together and dried in the sun to "form a whip as tough and hard as whalebone," which wounded with every blow and could easily be handled by a woman or child.[9] Woolrich, speaking of Tortola, declared that

> "most of the field–negroes are marked by the whip; all that he had seen, work under the whip, which the drivers carry for their correction, and of which they are continually in dread. It is made generally of plaited cowskin, with thick strong lashes; a formidable instrument in the overseers' hands, who would take the skin off a horse's back with one of them; (I have) seen them lay its marks into a deal board."[10]

Flogging was the common punishment for every offense and was often carried to excess. The *Authentic History* records that

> "For a trifling failure of duty, thirty–nine lashes are considered sufficient; when crime claims greater punishment, the number of lashes are encreased to one hundred, or as many more as caprice directs."[11]

Caines knew planters who "talk of 'a cool hundred,' and of 'peeling their slaves,' as if these were witticisms."[12]

The crimes which might exact the penalty of flogging or even more hideous punishments including the stealing of a plantain, or a yam, or a glass of rum.[13] Caines wrote that, "If the boy in waiting, the orderly man, brought his master's shoes, dirty at the toe or at the heel, he was flogged, severely flogged. . .."[14] Equiano said, "I have seen a Negro beaten till some of his bones were broken, for only letting a pot boil over."[15] Another author, arguing that punishment was often imposed not to correct but "to gratify a vindictive spirit," reported that, "I have known negroes flogged without knowing for what offense."[16]

> The punishment was administered, as he had seen, while "The culprit, either man or woman, is tied to a tree or held down by four men, each holding an arm or leg. During this infliction the planter looks on with calm indifference, as if deaf to the piercing shrieks which almost rend the air."[17]

He had known a planter's lady to order her negro driver "to flog a female slave, chiefly across the bosom."[18]

Flogging, of course, was not the only punishment imposed upon the slaves by their owners. The means of torture were many and varied, and included use of the stocks, ball and chain, thumb screws, being made to stand on one foot over a sharp stick, imprisoning in coffin–like boxes, requiring the wearing of a triangular iron about the neck—which prevented the victim from lying down to rest, amputation of arms or legs, roasting over a rum distilling furnace, hanging from a hook passed through the ribs, quartering by horses, burning alive and being left hanging on a gibbet to starve and die.

The owners of slaves who were executed after judicial sentence were recompensed out of the public treasury, the Virgin Islands Slave Act of 1783 specifying a maximum indemnity of £50.[19] One governor of the Leeward Islands had complained to London that "payment for negroes executed" was "a very large article" of the expenses of his government.[20]

Fatal floggings and death by torture were not the only dangers threatening slaves who offended their white masters. Simple murder was another. The *Authentic History* commented on the fate of slaves who crossed their overseers:

> "Should a luckless slave, in an evil hour, offend the manager, his death is certain, though various the means by which it is worked: sometimes, he is ordered to attend him when shooting; the unsuspecting negro, early discovers the game, but, instead of the bird that is started, himself is the victim, and he is shot dead on the spot. Conscience troubles not the overseer, and, but for the fear of incurring his employer's displeasure, he would boast of killing the black dog."[21]

Thomas Woolrich testified before Parliament that he knew of no protection that slaves had from mistreatment by their masters. He recounted an instance in which a runaway negro on Tortola was found asleep in one of his master's huts by an overseer who had been sent out to take him dead or alive. The overseer "shot him through the body. The negro, jumping up, said, 'What, you kill me asleep!' and dropt dead immediately. The overseer took off his head and carried it to his owner."[22]

He also knew of a planter who, irritated with his mulatto waiting man, reached for his gun and shot him through the head.[23]

The manager of a Tortola estate, whose owner was not living on the island at the time, "sitting at dinner, in sudden resentment, ran his cook, a negroe woman, through the body, and she died immediately. The negroes were called in to take her away and bury her."[24]

Woolrich observed that, "All the white people in the island were acquainted with these facts, which happened when he was in it, and which none doubted: neither of these offenders were ever called to an account, nor were they at all shunned or considered in disgrace."[25]

*   *   *

Torn from their families, their friends, their culture and all they had ever loved or ever owned; confined for many weeks in a prison ship which carried them across an ocean; sold; malnourished; overworked; brutalized; it is little wonder that many of the slaves gave way to despair.

The *Authentic History* reported that "Some, to avoid these dreadful punishments, have committed suicide: particularly the Coromantyn negroes, who frequently, while being flogged, threw back their heads in the neck and swallow their tongue, which chokes them instantaneously. Another painful method of shortening existence, is to eat common earth, whereby the stomach is prevented from performing its usual functions, and the sufferer lingers, in a state of most shocking debility, for a twelve–month."[26]

Woolrich testified that suicide was not common among the West Indian born Creole slaves but that he knew "of a good many (instances) among Africans." He told of six newly purchased African slaves who had been left alone on a small island off Tortola on a Saturday night and were all found hanging near together in the woods on Monday morning. Often, he told the members of Parliament, he "had inquired of the most sensible negroes what could be the cause of such actions, and the answer was, 'That they would rather die, than live in the situation they were in.'"[27]

Others, equally desperate, were despite the odds against them, driven to revolt. Major slave revolts had occurred from time to time in Jamaica, which, with its size and its mountains, offered some opportunity for escape in case of failure.[28] In Haiti, similarly situated, the slaves were to gain their freedom.[29] But the prospects of success or escape were not as great in the smaller, more compact islands, although in the Virgin Islands there was at least some prospect of escape to Puerto Rico—visible in the distant west from Tortola's mountain peaks—where the King of Spain offered freedom to the body in return for the conversion of the soul.[30]

In 1799 the Methodist missionaries had been accused of involvement in a revolt of some nature which took place on Tortola.[31] Earlier, in May 1790, the slaves on the estate left by the late Quaker deputy–governor, John Pickering, revolted. Dr. Lettsom had recorded how, twenty–two years earlier, they had clamored to honor Pickering one final time in death and, having paid their respects, left him with "silent, sullen, fixed melancholy."[32] His son, Isaac Pickering, had moved to England and the estate was now managed by Colonel Thomasons, his attorney, and other employees whose desire to report a profit to their employer in England was not tempered by the tenets of the Society of Friends. During a visit by Thomasons to the estate, he, the resident manager and the overseers, were attacked by the slaves, who "stoned them, and compelled them to take refuge in the house, which they repeatedly endeavoured to force. They continued stoning the house for hours, until assistance was procured from other estates, who liberated these gentlemen from their perilous situation, and guarded them in safety through the estate."[33]

President Turnbull of the Virgin Islands Council reported to Governor Shirley in Antigua that "by timely and spirited exertions and the diligent search made after them the whole gang (save one) were compelled to surrender, and five of the ringleaders after a fair and open Trial on Saturday last were severally Sentenced, Two for Execution and Three for Transportation. The former received their Doom (Monday) morning."[34]

Turnbull reported that the revolt grew from the belief, general among the slaves on the island, that they had been freed by the British government but that the news was being suppressed by the white inhabitants. "So much," he railed, "are we indebted to Mr. Wilberforce and his adherents."[35]

For slavery and—or at least—its cruelties were at long last, for a complex variety of altruistic and pragmatic reasons, being called into question. "Be but more lenient, oh! ye planters," the *Authentic History* closed, "use the correction of persuasion rather than the whip—so shall your sugar produce a sweeter flavor,—so shall your slaves serve you with the cheerfulness of willing obedience,—so shall abject fear vanish,—fear, which, like the gloomy tyrant, may enforce submission, but never obtains love."[36]

6

The Abolition of the Slave Trade: "It's So Odious"

Europeans began to enslave Africans before Columbus discovered the New World. The Portuguese were first, returning home with slave cargoes from their discoveries in sub-Saharan Africa in the 1440s. The first black slaves were taken to the New World from Spain in 1502, just ten years after Columbus' epoch voyage.[1] But even before then the native Americans had been reduced to slavery. The "Indian" population of the island known to the natives as Haiti and called by the Spaniards Hispaniola and that of the Bahamas had been forced, within a few years after 1492, to abandon their way of life so that they might labor in the mines and fields of the Spaniards.[2] Their treatment was atrocious—so much so that Bishop Bartolome de las Casas, their saintly protector, was to suggest the continued importation of a limited number of Africans to ease their burdens. It was a suggestion that he lived to repent.[3]

The slave trade continued for more than three hundred years, bringing misery to countless human beings. Gradually the bulk of the trade passed into British hands. Year in and year out ships sailed from Liverpool or Bristol to the western coast of Africa, thence to the West Indies and on back home having carried trade goods, human beings and sugar and rum in their triangular voyages.[4] By 1783 Lord North, George III's Prime Minister, would declare "that it would be found impossible to abolish the Slave Trade . . . for it was a trade which has in some measure become necessary to every nation in Europe."[5]

Not all shared his attitude. For many years the members of the Society of Friends, or Quakers, had shown an increasing aversion to the trade and to slavery itself.[6] Their founder, George Fox, had, as early as 1671, preached in Barbados that slaveholders had an obligation to treat their slaves with kindness, to "bring them to the knowledge of the Lord," and in due course set them free.[7] As early as 1696 the Pennsylvania Yearly Meeting spoke against the importation of slaves into the Quaker colony.[8] The London Yearly Meeting condemned the trade in 1727.[9] Similar resolutions were adopted in Pennsylvania in 1754 and in London in 1758.[10] In 1761 those "concerned in the unchristian traffic in negroes" were excluded from membership—a ban extended two years later to all who gave encouragement to the trade. In 1776 all Quakers who owned slaves were commanded to set them free.[11] As a consequence, in the Virgin Islands, slaves were freed and given property by Quaker owners in Tortola, Guana and Great Camanoe.[12]

While the Quakers had been condemning slavery in the colonies the institution had spread to Britain itself. West Indian planters returning to England for extended visits or to live the lives of gentlemen off the profits of their estates frequently brought personal servants with them. In England they might continue as valets, coachmen, cooks or what have you, be rented out for labor or even sold and returned to the West Indies. Some ran away. Others —grown infirm—were put out to fend for themselves.[13]

By 1770 there were an estimated 14,000 to 15,000 slaves in England.[14] Their status seemed settled by a joint opinion of the Attorney General and the Solicitor General, obtained by the planter interest in 1729, holding that a slave entering Great Britain or Ireland did not thereby become free and could be returned to the West Indies against his will. They had added, "that baptism doth not bestow freedom on him, nor make any alteration in his temporal conditions in these kingdoms."[15]

Slavery was to be abolished in England through the almost

single–handed efforts of one of the great humanitarians of all time —Granville Sharp. A man of no great wealth, Sharp worked for eighteen years as a clerk in the Ordnance Office before resigning to show his dislike for the war against the American colonies. During that same period his avocation was Liberty.[16]

One day in 1765, while walking to the home of his brother William—a London surgeon with a reputation for charity to the poor—Sharp chanced upon a negro, Jonathan Strong, who was trying to locate William Granville. Strong had been badly beaten by his owner, David Lisle, a Barbadian planter, and put out to die. The Sharp brothers arranged for his hospitalization and, upon his release, found him a job. Two years later Lisle spotted Strong on a London street. Realizing that he had thrown away a valuable property, Lisle had him kidnapped and sold to a planter who was soon to leave for Jamaica. Strong managed to get word of his plight to Granville Sharp. Sharp, with the help of the Lord Mayor of London, obtained a court hearing at which Strong was ordered released on the ground that he had been arrested without a warrant.[17]

Pleased with the result in Strong's case but troubled by the fragility of the narrow ground on which his friend had obtained his release, Sharp commenced a two year study of the law relating to slavery. In 1769 he published his conclusion that there was no legal basis for slavery in England and distributed copies of his work widely. In the meantime he sought and found other cases to test his position in court, each time obtaining freedom for his client but always upon a technical ground applicable only to the individual case before the court.[18]

Then, in 1771, the situation of James Somerset was brought to his attention. Somerset had been born in Africa, enslaved, and eventually became the property of a Virginian, Charles Stewart, who brought him to England. Having escaped, he was recaptured and put aboard a ship bound for Jamaica to be sold. Sharp saw his case as clearly presenting the issue he was attempting to test—whether a slave obtained freedom by living in England.[19]

Somerset v. Stewart[20] bears an obvious resemblance to more recent great legal contests of its genre in which much more has been at stake than the rights and duties of the named plaintiffs and defendants. As with its American counterpart—*Scott vs. Sandford,*[21] the Dred Scott decision which would lead to the bloodiest civil war the world had known—and *Brown v. Board of Education,*[22] which would fundamentally alter race relations in America, the case of Mr. Stewart's slave attracted nationwide attention and interest. The facts not being in dispute—as Granville Sharp had wished—all attention was focused on the question of law phrased by Somerset's counsel: Is England a country "whose air is deemed too pure for slaves to breathe in it?"[23]

The case was heard in the court of King's Bench by the Chief Justice, Lord Mansfield, who had decided to hear it alone rather than convoking a panel of judges. Mansfield realized the importance of the decision he was called upon to make and shrank from it, but the die was cast.

The court heard arguments on several occasions in the winter and spring of 1772. The barristers appearing on behalf of Somerset began by defining and narrowing their case. It only concerned the present, not what the law may once have been. It only concerned Somerset's status in England, not what it might be in the American and West Indian colonies.

The lawyers argued about the ancient state of villenage or serfdom in England, the history of slavery, the status of slaves in other countries and the extent to which colonial law ought to be given force in England.[24] Great concern was expressed as to the economic consequences of a judgment freeing Somerset. At the close of the arguments, on May 14, Lord Mansfield summed up, declaring,

> "The question is, if the owner had a right to detain the slave, for the sending of him over to be sold in Jamaica. In five or six cases of this nature I have known it to be accommodated by agreement between the parties. On it's first coming before

me, I strongly recommended it here. But if the parties will
have it decided, we must give our opinion. Compassion will
not, on the one hand, nor inconvenience on the other be to
decide, but the law. . .. The setting 14,000 or 15,000 men
at once free loose by a solemn opinion, is much disagreeable
in the effects it threatens. . .. [But] if the parties will have
judgment, *fiat justitia, ruat coelum*, let justice be done whatever the consequence. . .."[25]

Then, complimenting the young gentlemen of the bar on the
excellence of their arguments and again urging settlement, he put
the case over for decision.[26]

That decision was rendered on June 22, 1772. Mansfield briefly
recited Somerset's history and recapitulated the arguments which
had been made to him. Then, concluding, he declared,

"The only question before us is, whether the cause on the
return [of the writ of habeas corpus] is sufficient? If it is, the
negro must be remanded; if it is not he must be discharged.
Accordingly, the return states that the slave departed and
refused to serve; whereupon he was kept, to be sold abroad.
So high an act of dominion [over another] must be recognized by the law of the country where it is used. The power
of a master over his slave has been extremely different in
different countries. The state of slavery is of such a nature,
that it is incapable of being introduced on any reasons,
moral or political; but only positive law, which preserves its
force long after the reasons occasion, and time itself from
whence it was created is erased from memory [can support
it]. It's so odious, that nothing can be suffered to support it,
but positive law. Whatever inconveniences, therefore, may
follow from a decision, I cannot say this case is allowed or
approved by the law of England; and therefore the black
must be discharged."[27]

"It's so odious . . . the black must be discharged." James Somerset would not be returned to Jamaica. A precedent had been set and the opponents of slavery had won their first victory.

*   *   *

Sharp marked his victory by writing to the Prime Minister, Lord North, urging that the Government abolish the slave trade and free all slaves in the British colonies. King George's minister did not reply.[28]

Undaunted, Sharp continued his crusade of education and exposition. In 1783 he brought to the attention of the British public the notorious case of the slave ship *Zong*.[29] The *Zong*, out of Liverpool, had sailed from Africa to Jamaica with a cargo of 440 slaves, and a crew of fourteen whites. Luke Collingwood, her captain, having mistaken the coast of Jamaica for that of Hispaniola, sailed too far to the west and had to work back against the winds. In the meantime dysentery had broken out and sixty of the slaves and half of the fourteen whites had died.

Captain Collingwood realized that the voyage would a financial loss. Under the terms of the insurance policy covering the voyage, the loss of slaves dying on board ship fell upon the owners, but should it become necessary to throw any overboard "for the preservation of the ship" the loss would fall upon the insurance underwriters. Collingwood, who had an interest in the voyage, therefore persuaded his remaining crew members to join in shifting the loss to the underwriters. This was done by bringing up the slaves from the hold and throwing them overboard to drown. Fifty–four were disposed of the first day; forty–two the second, twenty–six, in irons, the third. Ten others threw themselves into the sea.

In due course the claim for insurance led to litigation. The owners claimed that the 132 slaves had been drowned to preserve water for their remaining fellows and that the drowning had therefore been "necessary" under the terms of the policy. The underwriters claimed that there had been water enough and that the slaves had been drowned in a fraudulent attempt to collect on the insurance policy. The case was tried before Lord Mansfield and a jury, which returned a verdict for the owners. Mansfield, considering a motion for a new trial, declared,

> "The matter left to the jury is 'was it from necessity?' —for they had no doubt (though it shocks one very much) that the case of slaves, was the same as if horses had been thrown overboard!! It is a very shocking case."[30]

He granted a new trial, which resulted in a verdict for the underwriters.

Sharp attended the trials and hired a shorthand reporter to transcribe the evidence which he then presented to the Lords of the Admiralty, the First Lord of the Treasury, the Prime Minister and the press, demanding that those responsible for the drownings be tried for murder. Nothing happened.[31] But Sharp had made his point. A month later the Quakers presented a petition to Parliament, calling for the abolition of the slave trade.[32] The stage had been set for a national debate on the trade.

The Quakers followed their petition with the establishment of a Meeting for Sufferings, whose purpose it was to publicize the evils of slavery and the trade.[33] The next year James Ramsey, who had served for almost twenty years as an Anglican minister on the island of St. Kitts, published, shortly after his return to England, his description of slavery as it was practiced in the islands and his prescription for a gradual emancipation which would, in the long run, best secure not only the moral but the economic interests of both Britain and the colonies. The planter interest denounced Ramsey and his proposals, continuing an acrimonious public debate with him until his death in 1789.[34]

In the year following the publication of Ramsey's book the subject selected for the Prize Latin Essay at Cambridge University was "Anne liceat invitos in servitutem dare?—Is it right to make slaves of others against their will?" The prize was won by Thomas

Clarkson, then twenty–five, who—deeply troubled by the information he had gathered in preparing his essay—was to devote more than half a century to the battles for abolition and emancipation. Riding back to London from Cambridge after receiving his prize, he dismounted and—in a scene reminiscent of the conversion of St. Paul,

> sat down disconsolate on the turf by the roadside and held my horse. Here a thought came into my mind that, if the contents of the essay were true, it was time some person should see these calamities to their end."[35]

Student essays rarely lead to such results.

Clarkson translated his Latin essay into English and published it as "An Essay on the Slavery and Commerce of the Human Species, particularly the African." Soon he had met Sharp, Ramsey and the Quaker abolitionists. In May 1787 the Quaker committee was reconstituted to include two non-Quakers—Granville Sharp and Thomas Clarkson—and renamed the Society for Effecting the Abolition of the Slave Trade.[36] The Society set about a massive propaganda campaign, including the distribution of a plaque designed by Josiah Wedgwood featuring a figure of a chained, kneeling black and the inscription "AM I NOT A MAN AND A BROTHER?"

The same design was used on trade tokens—then substituting for official pennies—issued throughout the country. The Society also entered into correspondence with similar organizations in France, headed by Robespierre, and in America, headed by Benjamin Franklin.

Seal of the Society for Effecting the Abolition of the Slave Trade,
designed by Josiah Wedgwood

Clarkson had already met William Wilberforce, the wealthy, young, charming Member of Parliament for Hull in Yorkshire. Wilberforce had been elected to Parliament at the age of twenty–one, in 1780, and was a close friend of William Pitt, the Prime Minister, who had achieved that office in 1783, at the age of twenty–four. In 1785 Wilberforce had undergone a religious experience of unusual depth. Troubled by doubts about his future and the purpose of his life, Wilberforce had sought out the rector of St. Mary Woolnoth, London, John Newton.[37] Newton (famous today as the composer of the hymn "Amazing Grace") was a remarkable character. He had gone to sea in the slave trade as a youth and wound up himself a slave on an island off the African coast. Rescued, he eventually became the captain of a slave ship. Converted, he preached to his crews of the mercies of the crucified Lord. Then, gradually enlightened, he took Holy Orders and had become a battler against the trade. His impact on the young par-

liamentarian was enormous. Wilberforce told Pitt of his conversion and of his concern with the trade.[38] "Pitt," Wilberforce was
to recollect, "recommended to me to undertake its conduct as a
subject suited to my character and talents. At length . . . I resolved
to give notice, on a fit occasion, in the House of Commons, of my
intention to bring the matter forward."[39]

Before that could be done, Clarkson and Wilberforce agreed,
Wilberforce had to have *facts* concerning the trade which would
withstand the scrutiny of parliamentary debate. Clarkson then
spent five months visiting Bristol and Liverpool, collecting first
hand information on the harshness of the trade and the conditions
under which the sailors who were enticed into it lived. Clarkson
and the Society reported to Wilberforce and Pitt, including in
their report a plan of a slave ship illustrating the crowded conditions under which the slaves existed for weeks at a time. Pitt then
consulted Ramsey and, convinced that not enough evidence was
yet at hand, ordered the Privy Council to report on the trade.[40]

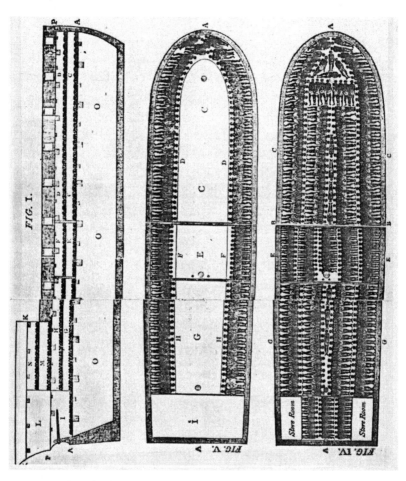

Plan of a Slave Ship

While the Council's report was being prepared Parliament took the first step toward ameliorating the conditions in the trade by adopting a bill offered by Sir William Dolben, member for Oxford University, limiting the number of slaves who could be carried in a ship and rewarding the masters and surgeons of ships when the mortality rate on a Middle Passage voyage was less than three percent. Similar and somewhat stronger measures were adopted in subsequent years. During the 1790s the mortality rate on British slave ships was to decline by more than a half.[41]

The Privy Council's report was submitted to Parliament early in 1789 and on May 12 Wilberforce obtained a vote condemning the trade in the Commons. It was determined that the shipping and West Indian interests should be allowed to present their case and the Select Committee before which Thomas Woolrich testified about conditions in Tortola heard evidence until the spring of 1791.[42]

On April 18, 1791, Wilberforce moved in the Commons for the immediate abolition of the slave trade. Despite all the preparation and the support of Pitt, Edmund Burke and Charles James Fox, the measure failed.[43] The next year the Commons passed a bill setting January 1, 1796, as the date for ending the trade, but the bill was not considered by the House of Lords.[44]

Meanwhile, the French Revolution had come to the Caribbean and, particularly, to St. Domingue, France's richest sugar colony. There the slaves rose in rebellion and, amid blood and flames, established the independent state of Haiti. Fear that tinkering with the existing system would lead to similar events in the British Caribbean islands and the preoccupations of Britain's war with France cooled the national zeal for abolition and emancipation. For several years more Wilberforce continued to raise the abolition issue in each session of Parliament but met increasing opposition from the well–represented West Indian interests who had organized to protect their economic interests and way of life.[45] One argument against immediate abolition advanced by the West Indians was that the lot of the slaves could be best improved by the planters themselves. If, following such improvement, the slave population then began to reproduce itself there would be not further need for the slave trade and it could be abolished without destroying the profitable trade in sugar.[2]

In 1797 the West Indian interests succeeded in getting the Commons to adopt a resolution urging the King to direct his governors in the West Indies to recommend to their local legislatures that they adopt measures "to obviate the causes which have hitherto impeded the natural increase of the Negroes already in the Islands," lead to the eventual termination of the slave trade, "employ such means as may conduce to the moral and religious improvement of the Negroes" and secure to them the protection of the law.[46]

This resolution was duly transmitted by the Governor of the Leeward Islands to the five colonies in his jurisdiction—Antigua, Montserrat, Nevis, St. Christopher and the Virgin Islands. The Councils and Assemblies of Antigua and St. Christopher responded by urging the Governor to convene the General Council and General Assembly of the Leeward Islands. These venerable bodies, relics of an early attempt at federation, were convened for the first time in seventy–five years. The appointed Councils of each of the five colonies named two members to serve in the General Council and the freeholders of each colony elected five members to serve in the General Assembly. The federal legislature met on March 1, 1798.[47]

On the opening day of the session Governor Robert Thomson addressed the representatives of the four island colonies present (the members from the Virgin Islands were to arrive two weeks late and leave before the legislature had completed its work). Touching on his forty years' residence in the islands, he spoke of the English Parliament's resolution and of the gradual improvement in the lot of the slaves which he had seen in his lifetime, declaring that,

"The increase of our Negroes by propagation, rather than by importation, is an object to be wished for by us all, who know the superior value of Creole Negroes to those imported from Africa; and, surely, to every humane mind it must prove an object of the most pleasing contemplation, to behold his Gang thriving and increasing under his fostering hand. I am therefore persuaded, you will devote your attention to the removal of every kind of impediment, that may appear to you to stand in the way of accomplishing so desirable an object.

"If the Legislature of the Parent State have wisely abandoned the idea of a forced and abrupt abolition of the Slave Trade, and wish to see whether it can be gradually accomplished by natural means, let us, on our part, do everything in our power to try the experiment fairly."[48]

The General Assembly and General Council adjourned eight weeks later, having produced the Leeward Islands Melioration Act: "An Act [as it was titled] more effectually to provide for the Support, and to extend certain Regulations for the Protection of Slaves, to promote and encourage their Increase, and generally to meliorate their Condition."[49]

This act, which was approved by the Crown on March 6, 1799, carefully regulated the provisions which were to be provided to the slaves, specifying in detail basic weekly diets ranging from nine pints of corn to thirty pounds of bananas, together with a pound and a quarter of salted, or two and a half pounds of fresh fish.[50] Provision grounds were also to be allotted to the slaves on which they could grow their own crops.[51]

The hours of the day were regulated, with a half hour provided for breakfast and two hours for dinner.[52] No work was to be done before five in the morning or after seven in the evening, except in crop time or "from some evident necessity."[53]

In January and August the owner was to provide each of his male slaves with a jacket and trousers and each of his female slaves with a wrapper and petticoat. A blanket could, with the slave's consent, be substituted for the clothing.[54] Medical and spiritual care was to be provided.[55] The slaves were encouraged to select single husbands or wives, although they were denied religious rites of marriage "lest the violation of sacred vows be too often added to the crime of infidelity."[56]

The Act was to "always be favourably construed . . . as will best tend to promote and secure the protection and comfort of slaves"[57] and not to be construed as preventing the individual colonial legislatures from enacting more liberal measures.[58]

Article XXI provided:

> "That every White or free Coloured–Person charged with the murder or maiming of any slave, whether such slave belong to such person or not, shall be tried and punished for such murder or maiming in the same manner, without any sort of distinction or privilege, as if he or she were charged with the murder or maiming of any white or free person whatever."

*   *   *

The first European nation to abolish the trade in slaves to its American possessions was Denmark, which after ten years of preparation ended the trade to its Virgin Island colonies of St. John, St. Thomas and St. Croix on January 1, 1803.[59]

In the United States President Jefferson used the occasion of his 1806 State of the Union message to urge the abolition of the slave trade upon the expiration of the Constitution's twenty–year ban on interference with it. Congress responded by outlawing the trade as of January 1, 1808.[60]

Wilberforce, in Britain, had ceased his annual parliamentary efforts for several sessions. He renewed them in 1804, when the Commons passed his bill to abolish the trade forthwith, although the House of Lords postponed consideration of the issue.[61] The following year, to his surprise, Wilberforce's bill was defeated by a sparsely–attended Commons on a vote of 77 to 70.[62]

Wilberforce then turned to Pitt, still the Prime Minister, for a step toward partial abolition. In 1803 Britain, in the course of the Napoleonic wars, had captured the Dutch colonies in Guyana. Wilberforce and his allies now prevailed upon Pitt to issue, on August 15, 1805, an Order–in–Council prohibiting the importation of slaves into the occupied Dutch colonies.[63] This was followed, in 1806, by passage of the Foreign Slave Trade Bill which prohibited British slavers from selling their cargoes in either foreign or occupied ports.[64] As much as three–quarters of the British slave trade was destroyed by the passage of this bill.[65]

The stage was now set for the final parliamentary battle. This time the first round would be fought in the House of Lords. Pitt had died in early 1806 and was followed in office by Lord Grenville, a supporter of the abolitionist cause. The Prime Minister himself introduced the abolition bill in the House of Lords on January 2, 1807.[66] The bill was shepherded through the House of Lords by Lord Auckland, brother–in–law of Hugh Elliot, the future Governor of the Leeward Islands,[67] and passed, despite the opposition of the Duke of Clarence (the future King William IV)[68] by a vote of 100 to 34.[69] The way was now clear for action by the Commons, which passed the bill by a vote of 283 to 16[70] and sent it on for the Royal Assent, which was received on March 25th.[71]

The long struggle to abolish the British slave trade was at an end. No slave ship was to clear a port of the United Kingdom after May 1, 1807, nor deliver human cargo to the colonies after March 1, 1808.[72]

But slavery persisted.

Arthur Hodge
By courtesy of the National Portrait Gallery, London

7

Arthur Hodge:
"Great Accomplishments and Elegant Manners"

During the last years of the parliamentary fight to abolish the slave trade Arthur William Hodge was living on Tortola, where he had been born in 1763.[1] His father, for whom he was named, had been a wealthy planter who became a member of the island's governing Council.[2] The family appears to have moved to Tortola from Anguilla during the migration in the early decades of the century.[3] It included at least one daughter, Anne, who was to marry John Rawbone of Tortola.

Arthur had the upbringing of a child of the West Indian gentry. He most likely was sent to England for education at an early age.[4] At eighteen he entered Oriel College of Oxford University.[5]

A year later, in November 1782, Arthur entered the Army as a Second Lieutenant in the Royal Welch Fusiliers (23rd Foot). The Fusiliers were one of the regiments which had surrendered a year earlier to Washington's army at Yorktown and most of the members of the regiment were still imprisoned awaiting the conclusion of the peace treaty which was then being negotiated in Paris. An officer entering the regiment in 1782 would, most likely, have remained in England recruiting new soldiers to rebuild the regiment. Hodge was mustered out of the regiment at the end of 1783.[6]

At the time of his death Arthur Hodge would be described as "a man of great accomplishments and elegant manners."[7]

Hodge was twenty–four when he was appointed to membership in the Virgin Islands' Council by Sir Thomas Shirley, Governor of the Leeward Islands, and took the oath of office as a member of the upper house of the legislature and a Justice of the Peace at Roadtown, Tortola, in November 1787.[8] However, for some reason the Crown did not immediately confirm him in office and, having returned to England, he enlisted parliamentary aid in petitioning for confirmation of his appointment. He again requested confirmation in August 1790 when he was back in Tortola.[9] It was finally given in June 1791.[10]

Like many West Indian planters, Hodge probably spent many of the following years in England. He had already wed and lost one wife when he married Jane MacNamara, who gave him a daughter, Rosina Jane, about 1795.[11] Jane must have died shortly afterwards. She may have been a daughter of the Member of Parliament who had assisted him in obtaining confirmation of his appointment to the Council.[12]

During the late 1790s, as the wars spawned by the French Revolution raged through the Caribbean, Hodge was back in Tortola. There he must have watched with concern the approach of a French squadron which sailed into the harbor at Roadtown. Luckily, the French, learning of the strength of the militia, which had been augmented through the arming of the Christian blacks with the cooperation of the Methodist missionaries, did not attempt a landing.[13] In 1798 a British naval sloop and a French privateer fought an engagement off Virgin Gorda and the victorious Captain Fahie of the Royal Navy brought his prize into Roadtown.[14]

While war continued the widowed Hodge found solace in the arms of his slave Peggy. In the year of Fahie's victory Peggy bore him a daughter, who was named Bella.[15]

The islands, slave mistresses and mulatto children could only hold Arthur Hodge so long. By 1800 he was back in England and in May of that year entered into a contract intended to provide a property settlement for his next wife.[16] The identity of the other parties to this agreement illuminates the position which he had obtained in English and West Indian society. In it he conveyed in trust his 535 acre plantation in Road Division of Tortola, with "all buildings, negroes, slaves and cattle" to procure his intended a £500 annual income in the event of his death. The trustees to whom the estate was conveyed were William Payne Georges of Manchester Square, London, and Captain William Charles Fahie of the Royal Navy.[17]

Georges was a son of the Chief Justice of St. Kitts and a nephew of Ralph Payne, Lord Lavington, Governor of the Leeward Islands.[18] Payne had served as Governor from 1771 to 1775 and again from 1798. He would remain in office until his death in 1807. This extraordinary man, who had long served in the British House of Commons and whose London hospitality inspired the horrid pun "he never knew pleasure who never knew Payne," was surrounded as Governor "by an army of servants, but he would not allow any of the black servitors about him to wear shoes or stockings, their legs being rubbed daily with butter so that they shone like jet; and he would not, if he could avoid it, handle a letter or parcel from their fingers. To escape the indignity, he designed a golden instrument, like a tongs, with which he held any article which was given him by a black servant."[19]

William Payne Georges' wife Ruth was a granddaughter and heiress of Bazaliel Hodge, who had accumulated fifteen estates on Tortola before his death in 1787. She was, undoubtedly, one of the wealthiest Virgin Islanders. Their London home was in fashionable Manchester Square.[20]

Fahie, the other trustee for the Hodge marriage settlement, was a son of John Fahie, who had served for many years as Speaker of the Assembly of St. Kitts, Acting Governor of the Virgin Islands and, after the institution of constitutional government, as President of the Virgin Islands.[21] Two years later Captain Fahie would be appointed to the Council of St. Kitts.[22]

A witness to the marriage settlement was Henry Cecil, then Earl and later Marquess of Exeter, the brother–in–law of the bride–to–be, Ann Hoggins.

The marriage of Henry Cecil and Ann's sister, Sarah, the Countess of Exeter, had been a Cinderella story come true.[23] Although Henry was nephew and heir to the wealthy Earl of Exeter, his first wife humiliated him by running off with a clergyman. To escape this embarrassment, Henry Cecil disguised himself (in that era before tabloids and television), moved to the small Shropshire village of Bolas Magna, bought property and settled into the life of a gentleman farmer under the alias "John Jones." Eventually Jones married Sarah Hoggins, the seventeen year old daughter of a neighboring farmer. A year later he left for London "on business" (in fact to pursue an action for criminal conversation against his wife's lover and obtain a bill of divorce from Parliament) to which city, after a time, he invited Sarah. There, as John Jones, and without explanation, he persuaded her to go through a second marriage ceremony. They then returned to Bolas Magna.

Two years later John Jones read of the death of his uncle, the Earl, and started off at once with his wife on a journey to Burghley House in Rutland. What, she asked him, was this castle? "It is all yours," he replied, "and you are the Countess of Exeter."

In 1797, at the age of twenty–three and after three years as Countess of Exeter, Sarah Hoggins died in childbirth. She left three small children and, in addition, several brothers and a sister, Ann, all of whom were provided for by Lord Exeter.

On June 2, 1800, less than a month after the execution of their marriage contract, Arthur Hodge, then thirty–seven, and Ann Hoggins, twenty–one, were married at Clifton, Gloucestershire.[24] They returned to London, residing at 3, George Street, Manchester Square, and in February 1801 Ann gave birth to a daughter, Jane. Two more children were to follow: a son, Henry Cecil Hodge, and a second daughter, Justina.[25]

In 1803 Arthur Hodge returned to Tortola to personally superintend the management of his estate.[26] His family sailed with him.

His estate then included about 130 slaves.[27] Three years before, in October 1800, while Robert Green was attorney for Hodge
and Daniel Ross was managing the estate, the slaves, who had
been "well disposed" until that time wanted "privileges" which
Ross would not grant and two-thirds of them ran away. Upon
their return two weeks later, Ross "cartwhipped the whole with
moderation" and they returned to their obedience.[28] Perhaps this
incident had helped form Arthur Hodge's determination to return
to Tortola and resume personal administration of his property.

View of Roadtown Harbor from Mount Bellevue

The plantation to which Hodge brought his family was located on the side of Mount Bellevue, from which it took its name,
overlooking, to the west, the beautiful harbor of Roadtown and
the mountains which rise above it.[29] Magnificent views of the Sir
Francis Drake Channel and the surrounding islands met the eye in
all directions. The "great house" was high up on the hill, above
the works where Hodge's slaves ground his cane to release the liq-
uid sugar within. The territory touched the shore at Fish Bay, just
to the east of Fort Shirley.

The typical West Indian planter's "great house" of the early

Nineteenth Century was described as being two or three storeys high, built of timber on a brick foundation. Its windows were shuttered and curtained but rarely glazed; the interior walls were of fine woods; the furnishing throughout elegant. The bedrooms contained four–poster beds surrounded by gauze curtains or richly ornamented hammocks. The kitchen stood separate some distance from the great house. Water was supplied by wells and cisterns.[30]

The Hodge estate would also have included a number of small cabins for the slaves, as well as the mill and boiling house for the production of sugar and rum from cane.

Hodge, as a senior member of the Council, soon resumed his place of importance in the government of the Virgin Islands. A major problem which that government faced was the provision of currency for the daily internal trade of the islands. The principal currency which had circulated in the islands consisted of cut pieces of Spanish silver dollars—halves, quarters and bitts or eighths, together with the small copper coin called a Black Dog which the French minted for their West Indian colonies and which had become so popular throughout the region that it was counterfeited in England for export to the colonies. The dollar "passed current" in the Virgin Islands at a lower rate than in the other British colonies. The result was that no uncut Spanish coins circulated in the Virgin Islands and cut pieces were not intrinsically worth the amounts for which they passed. At last, as Lord Lavington reported to London, the small merchants and hucksters refused any longer to accept the overvalued cut pieces of coin. Lavington declared that,

> "The inconvenience and distress which ensued upon this combination exceeded every idea which could be formed on the occasion: but when it is considered that the Road Town of Tortola, like all West India towns, is entirely supplied with bread, fresh meat, poultry, vegetables, grass for the horses of the inhabitants, and all the smaller articles of daily consumption, by the Negroes living in different parts of the country, it was evident that the absolute want of any

medium through which this traffic could be carried on,
would occasion an immediate dearth of every necessary of
life; for no Negro would bring his grass, or the produce of
his ground to market, while the only coin in which he could
be paid for it would not pass current with the only persons
who possessed the articles (provisions and clothing) of which
he might stand in need."[31]

The Legislature responded to the emergency by passing an act
legitimizing the circulation of £2,000 worth of cut coins, calling them
in to be stamped with the word TORTOLA or the initial "T".[32]

Private issues of currency also appeared and it must have been
about this time and after Hodge's return to Tortola that Black
Dogs bearing the initial "H" were put into circulation. These appeared in two forms, with the "H" enclosed by a square or a loz-
enge, and were to circulate for many years. Their appearance certainly marks Arthur Hodge as a dominant figure in the island
community.[33]

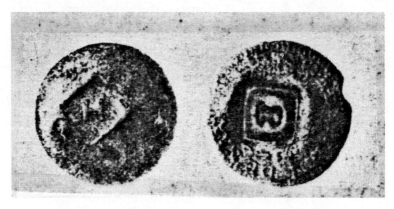

French Colonial "Black Dog" Coins Counter-stamped "H" for
"Hodge"

Hodge was also to become involved in religious dispute. He
had some sympathy for the new society of Methodists—a sympathy which was perhaps not surprising in a community whose only

Anglican clergyman had sailed off to command a privateer and involve himself in the Haitian wars.[34]

Brownell, the Methodist missionary on Tortola, wrote home that the Methodist chapel was the only place of worship on all the islands from Anageda to Jost van Dyke, adding, "I find religion has made a great alteration for the better among the blacks, but among the whites, fornication, adultery, and neglect of all religion are reigning sins." An extract of this letter, published in the *Methodist* magazine in August 1805, made its way back to Tortola and, as Brownell reported,

> "In consequence of this, a magistrate, [a Devonshire] clergyman's son, and two more, fell upon me in the open street, beat me unmercifully, and laid open my head with the butt end of a whip; they would certainly have killed me that day, but Providence by a little circumstance preserved me; and I carried my life in my hand for many weeks after."

Brownell accused his attackers in the Court of Grand Sessions. The Grand Jury refused to bring an indictment and ordered Brownell to pay costs "for bringing a matter frivolous and vexatious before this court." Then it proceeded to indict Brownell "for writing a libel on the community," although his allegations were acknowledged to be true.

The magistrate who had assaulted the missionary now sat on the bench to judge him and the prosecution asked that since it was not ready for trial he be thrown into prison until the next session of the court. At this point Hodge intervened, offering to stand bail for Brownell and the indictment against him was quashed.[35]

Brownell closed his report of the incident by observing that "this outrage did not alter the fact that there was neither church nor public worship: so to roll away the reproach, they began to read prayers in the court house, and have since built a church."[36]

Having offered to stand bail for the missionary, Arthur Hodge may well have contributed funds for the building of the church.

8

Death on Mount Bellevue:
"That Modern Golgotha"

In September 1805, Hodge hired a new manager for his plantation, one Stephen McKeough.[1] McKeough, who had been born in Ireland, had immigrated to the neighboring island of St. Thomas in 1800.[2] He was described by George Davis Dix, who had employed him as manager of his plantation at Ballast Bay on the west side of Tortola, as an "active, industrious man." Nevertheless, Dix had felt obliged to dismiss him for "intemperance" some months before Hodge hired him.[3]

McKeough, who was to serve Hodge on three separate occasions and stayed with him this first time for a period of six months, observed that when he first went to Bellevue to live Hodge had "a fine gang of negroes."[4]

A second occasional resident of Bellevue at about the same time was Perreen Georges, a mulatto ex–slave who did work for Mrs. Hodge and managed the boiling house. Perreen lived in town but would stay in "the white peoples' house" on the Hodge estate for a few days or weeks at a time.[5]

The Leeward Islands Melioration Act required that a log be kept of the slaves on each estate.[6] McKeough found that Hodge insisted that slaves whom he had been told were dead be marked on the list board as runaways.[7] McKeough soon learned why.

The slave woman Violet, together with her young son, had been purchased by Hodge in St. Thomas and brought to Tortola.

She was employed as a house servant at Bellevue, with the boy being put to work as a groom. As time passed, Hodge grew convinced that his new house slave was making a habit of stealing candles. He had her flogged and locked up, then flogged several more times. The boy, having been beaten, ran away and when he returned was put in chains and flogged repeatedly. Both Violet and her son were soon dead.[8]

By the end of 1805 conditions on the Hodge plantation had grown intolerable for many of the slaves. They were, as a result, more and more inclined to run way. Hodge employed other of his slaves as "hunters" to bring them back. Among the hunters was Welcome, a strong, young man of twenty-five, worth in McKeough's opinion, the high price of forty joes or 320 Spanish dollars. In January Hodge sent Welcome out after a group of runaways. He returned four or five days later, empty-handed. Hodge, unwilling to accept his lack of success, had him cartwhipped and sent him back out.

Again failing in his mission, Welcome returned to the plantation, only to have the whip applied to sores already festering upon his body and be sent back out a third time. Returning once more without the runaways, Welcome was again cartwhipped and then put in heavy irons, with a pudding on each leg and a crook around his neck. He was allowed little or nothing to eat and at night was put in the stocks.

Hodge now offered to sell Welcome to McKeough for five joes or forty dollars. McKeough, feeling that Welcome could not survive the treatment he had received, refused the offer but volunteered to take Welcome to his house off the estate near the shore of Paraqueta Bay. They set off together, with Welcome's torn flesh, as McKeough noted, sticking to the seat of his breeches. Half way down the hill Welcome could not go on and, being unable to sit, laid down on his belly in the road. McKeough went on to the house. Hodge, learning that Welcome was not with McKeough, had him brought back up to Bellevue and cartwhipped.

The next morning McKeough went to Hodge and asked for

Welcome. Hodge disclaimed any knowledge of his whereabouts. McKeough never saw Welcome again.[9]

Hodge's cruelties extended even to the children on his plantation. He ordered his own natural daughter, Bella, now about eight years old, to be cartwhipped. McKeough saw him strike her over the head with a stick and, on other occasions, "kick her so violently in the lower part of her belly, as to send her several feet on the ground."[10]

Other mulatto children were "taken up by the heels and dipped into tubs of water . . . with their heads under water, to be kept until they stifled; then taken out and suffered to recover and breathe, and then immediately to be treated in the same manner, and so repeatedly treated, until they stagger and fall; when Hodge ordered them to be taken up and suspended to a tree by their hands tied together, and in such situation cartwhipped for some time at 'close quarters' as he calls it."[11]

Perreen Georges was passing the plantation's sick–house one day and, looking in, "saw a child about ten years of age, named Sampson [or Tamson], with the skin all off." Horrified, she asked the slave sick nurse "what was the matter with the child, in the name of God?" The nurse shook her hand at her, telling her to leave and that the master must not know that the child had been seen. Perreen soon learned "by general report on the estate from the Negroes that the child had been, by Hodge's order, dipped into a copper of boiling liquor."[12]

During this period Ann Hodge was carrying her last child; a daughter, Justina.[13]

Stephen McKeough moved on and off the estate, living part of the time with the mulatto shopkeeper, Thomas Crook.[14] On March 27, 1807, McKeough moved back to Bellevue.[15] Little had changed.

One day, within three weeks of his return to the estate, he was walking up the hill from the sugar works to the mansion house. Half-way up he heard the sound of the whip and, upon entering the yard, found Hodge presiding over the whipping of a new slave named Tom. The whip stopped when McKeough entered the yard. Its sound resumed when he left and could be heard for an hour. Two or three days later McKeough saw Tom's body, "all raw," being carried on a board from the sickhouse for burial.[16] Tom Boiler died the same way,[17] and Cuffy.[18] Perreen Georges saw Cuffy whipped at the works for over an hour without stopping, until "he was cut to pieces, and had no black skin upon him remaining from his hips to his hands."

*   *   *

Dueling—as a formal, ritualized practice, with its challenges, choice of weapons and locales, and "seconds" conveying messages between the opposing parties—is unknown today, virtually forgotten and difficult to understand. Yet, in the late 1700s and early 1800s it was an important fact of life for the "better classes" in the English–speaking world. Hugh Elliot, the future governor of the Leeward Islands and then British Ambassador to Denmark, fought a duel with his wife's lover in 1782. Abraham Lincoln, the future president of the United States, was caught up in the practice as late as 1842.[19] In 1804, the year after Arthur Hodge returned to Tortola for the last time, the vice–president of the United States ritually murdered the nation's first Secretary of the Treasury on a New Jersey bluff overlooking the Hudson and the growing borough of Manhattan and in 1809 the British Foreign Secretary was seriously wounded by a bullet fired by the War Secretary while their nation's armies were in the field facing Napoleon's troops.[20]

In the Caribbean society, in which the "code of honor" was paramount, in which "every white man is a gentleman, and has a right to honorary reparation by one of his white compeers,"[21] Arthur Hodge soon acquired a lasting reputation as a feared and notorious duelist.[22] No record exists of all whom he fought, but he may have killed the husband of Frances Pasea Robertson[23] and, in this year 1807, dueled with the lawyer, Simpson.[24]

His skill with his pistols[25] was to long protect him, and might have "till the whole of his slaves had miserably perished"[26] but for the appearance in the government of the Leeward Islands "of a man uncorrupted by colonial prejudice"[27] for "it would be almost as unsafe to a man's person, as his character, after having given . . . a provocation, to refuse a challenge."[28]

*   *   *

Three months after the Simpson duel Hodge's wrath turned on another of his slaves. Jupiter, about nineteen years old, having offended in some way, was "severely cartwhipped, and put in heavy irons, crook puddings, etc. and allowed little or nothing to eat." This time a new refinement was added—"he was burnt in the mouth with a hot iron." Jupiter, too, soon died.[29]

Among the house servants were Margaret and Elsey. Margaret's mother had nursed Hodge's sister, Anne. Margaret worked in the kitchen as a cook; Elsey was a washerwoman. Hodge, overseeing the deaths of others, grew fearful for his own life and kept a dagger at the head of his bed.[30] Now he began to imagine the deaths of his own "innocent babes," and conceived the notion that Margaret and Elsey were plotting to poison Mrs. Hodge and their children. Hodge determined to punish them as he had others and ordered kettles of boiling water prepared. Perreen did not have the heart to remain present, but heard Margaret's "screeches" as the boiling water was poured down her throat and saw both Margaret and Elsey running afterwards with scalded mouths. Cartwhipped and chained together, naked, Margaret and Elsey were delivered to McKeough to be put to work in the fields.

Margaret lingered, complaining always of the pain in her stomach and spitting blood. On Christmas Day, 1807, when Hodge's widowed sister Anne, who had shared the breast with Margaret, and her friend, Ann Arindell, were visiting the Hodges, she, together with Joan, was to cook the dinner. On Christmas morning Margaret was released from the chains in which she was kept in the sick–house and the suspected poisoner was sent to the mansion to take orders for dinner for the guests.

Margaret was chopping meat in the kitchen when Perreen entered. Observing that she was "stupid," Perreen told her so and asked what was the matter. Margaret pulled off the handkerchief which she wore about her head, revealing wounds in her forehead and in the back of her head; the one in back so large that three fingers could be laid in it. Hodge had given them to her, she said. Perreen told Margaret to leave off her work and prepared some rice for her to eat, which she could not take. Perreen took over the preparation of the dinner; which was about to be carried to the Great House dining room, when Margaret fell, face first, upon the floor. While Margaret was carried to the sick–house the Hodges and their guests praised the meal which they supposed she had prepared.

That night there was the sound of Negroes knocking at the door and of Arthur Hodge going out and returning. In the morning Perreen saw Margaret's coffin.[31]

The closing year had witnessed the deaths of other inhabitants of Bellevue. Little Simon, having been whipped at "close quarters"—that is, with the whip shortened so that it would wrap around, instead of crossing the body[32] —for a full half hour without interruption and with the marks of the hot iron on his raw lips, was gone.[33] One morning Gift, a teenager, had been whipped and sent into the fields in chains. Whipped again after his labor, he died during the night.[34] The boy Dick had stolen a goose and run away. He was brought home, flogged, burnt on the mouth with the hot iron and flogged day after day again until he died.[35]

Peter, a free black, had been hired by Hodge as a cooper, building the barrels in which his sugar would be shipped to England, in return for his clothes, food and two joes a month. Notwithstanding his free status, he was whipped, chained and sent to work in the fields. Peter was soon dead.[36]

The new year, 1808—the year in which the slave trade ended—saw more of the same. Cudjo died in the same way as the others,[37] and others whose names are lost.[38]

Prosper, "a good looking, strong negro," who Hodge had previously stoned in an argument about a bull, saw a mango fall from a tree and picked it up. Hodge, considering the mango—like all else about him—his property, demanded that Prosper pay him the exorbitant sum of six shillings for it. Having no money, and terrified, Prosper ran to Perreen Georges at the sugar works and asked to borrow the six shillings. She offered him the three shillings she had, which he brought to Hodge.

Not satisfied, Hodge had him held down by four negroes and flogged with a cartwhip for over an hour, then told him to produce the remaining three shillings by the next day or face the same punishment again. The next day, within sight of the house, Prosper—not having the three shillings still due for the mango—was tied to a tree and whipped at short quarters so long that "he had no black skin upon him" and "could not bawl out any longer." Finally he was cut down, carried to the sick house and put in irons. Five days later his two companions in chains managed to break away. Prosper, too weak to escape, with "crawlers" in his wounds, and blue flies all about him, hid in his own cabin.

The "crawlers" were described by an English visitor to the West Indies, who had followed the case of a woman who had been severely beaten after her husband had been whipped and clubbed to death. He reported that

"One morning, upon hearing the loud cries of a female, I was led to look out at my window, when I saw some Negroes carrying this unfortunate woman from the sick–house into the yard, where they laid her down in the dirt, upon the bare ground, amidst a heavy shower of rain; then kneeling at her sides, they proceeded to examine minutely into her wounds: and you scarcely hold it credible, when I tell you that they were employed for a full half–hour *picking maggots out of her sores*.!!! The ulcerations had penetrated to a great depth, particularly withinside the thighs, where the lashes of the whips had cut round, and torn the flesh in a frightful manner. The ulcers were very raw and considerably enlarged, by the gnawing of the maggots which had been bred within them."

Alone, unattended, Prosper died. The stench coming from his cabin led to the discovery of his body, which was buried in a pit, without a coffin, at his back door.[39]

On November 29 Ann Hodge died.[40] It was said that one of her arms had been broken;[34] that "she died insane; her intellects, it was believed having been disordered by the shocking scenes she was forced to witness;"[35] that "she died of a fever."[36] Stephen McKeough, together with Daniel Ross, who was one of Hodge's fellow Justices and who had charge of his estate before he returned from England with his wife and children, dug her grave, "because there were no proper Negroes to do it."[37] Hodge, Ross and McKeough drank tea and dined together at the house that night.[38]

Ann Hoggins had been a girl of twelve back in Bolas Magna when her sister Sarah married the new gentleman–farmer neighbor, John Jones. She was fifteen when her sister suddenly became Countess of Exeter and eighteen when the Countess died. When twenty–one she had married her wealthy West Indian planter, Arthur Hodge, and had left England for the West Indies two years later. Now, at twenty–nine, she was dead.

Her white maid servant was also dead. It was said that she had miscarried and died as a result. Questions were asked as to whom she had called upon in her dying moments.[39]

Perreen Georges left the estate within the month.[40] Hodge's sister, Anne Collins, who was later to marry John Rawbone, left within the year, seeking "refuge" with Frances Pasea Robertson.[41] When Mrs. Robertson, whose son William was in England, remarked to her that they had no male protector and that "your brother may come with a side–saddle and take you away," she was surprised at Anne's reply, "Don't fear, 'tis more than he dare do— I could hang him."[42]

Stories were told, too, of a feud between Anne and Stephen McKeough.[43] McKeough was to leave Tortola in November 1809, going first to live in St. Thomas and then in St. Croix.[44] Hodge owed him £56 for past services when he left. When McKeough asked him for payment, "he threatened to cart–whip me." McKeough left with the debt unpaid.[45] He had lived off and on with Hodge for about three years. During that time Hodge had "lost sixty Negroes at least by the severity of his punishments;" only one had died a natural death —"Tom Driver, who died of the venereal complaint."[46]

Arthur Hodge had destroyed his capital. In August 1810 the Bellevue plantation was leased to the widow Ann McRae.[47]

9

Conflict and Accusation:
"Half-Uttered Threats"

An unlikely series of circumstances was to bring events in the Virgin Islands to the attention of the larger world.

William Payne Georges, the husband of Bazaliel Hodge's granddaughter Ruth and trustee of Arthur Hodge's marriage settlement, died in London in early 1806. He left his entire estate to his wife, to be joined to the vast estate which she had inherited from her grandfather.[1] It was estimated that her properties included over a thousand slaves and produced an annual income in excess of £10,000.[2] The administration of such properties would produce sufficient fees to pique the interest of more than one attorney and manager. Ruth was forty years of age when she lost her husband. After his death she returned to Tortola.

Dr. John Coakley Lettsom, always retaining his Quaker dress and mode of life, had enjoyed a long and distinguished career since, as a young man of twenty–three, he had left Tortola for the last time in 1768. He had gained fame as a physician, philanthropist and author. Although he resided in London and was never to return to the West Indies, Lettsom maintained his interest in the islands of his birth.

Lettsom's youngest son, Pickering Lettsom, a barrister of the Inner Temple, was sent to Tortola as a judge in 1808, when he was twenty–six. There he met the widow Ruth Georges, who was sixteen years his elder. Despite the differences in their ages, love bloomed and on September 22, 1808, they were married. But no sooner were they wed than the bridegroom was stricken ill and by October 28 he was dead. Ruth Lettsom was disconsolate at the death of her young husband and fell ill herself. Attended by Drs. William and John West (who also served the Arthur Hodge estate), she died on January 24, 1809.[3]

Although she was survived by a son and three daughters, Mrs. Lettsom had, during the brief period since her husband's death, made a will in which she left her wealth not to her children but to her father–in–law, John Coakley Lettsom. The estate was soon tied up in litigation, which would not be resolved until 1813.[4] In the meantime guardians and conservators would be needed to preserve and manage it.

William Musgrave, a young man from the island of Montserrat, was, like Pickering Lettsom, a barrister of the Inner Temple. Having practiced law in his native island for some time, he determined, for reasons he was later to regret, to move to Tortola in 1808. There he soon built a practice, often representing London merchants and clients from neighboring islands in suits against Virgin Islanders.[5]

Musgrave also soon gained appointment, upon the recommendation of Chief Justice James Robertson, to the position of King's Counsel. Although strictly an honorary title in England, the rank of King's Counsel carried with it, in the West Indies, the duty of acting as prosecuting officer for the Crown in the absence of higher law officers. More lucratively, the King's Counsel in Tortola customarily acted as advocate for the captors of foreign ships taken by privateers and presented for condemnation to the Vice Admiralty Court over which Robertson, wearing another hat, presided. Robertson's surrogate as judge of the prize court was Maurice Lisle. This was a bit irregular—even in the small community of the Virgin Islands in which every man of any ability seemed to hold several offices—as Lisle, American born, had served for the past twenty years as American agent in the Virgin Islands and carried on a continuing trade with the United States. The Customs officers of the neighboring islands (which included St. Thomas, St. John and St. Croix, taken from the Danes at the end of 1807) were said to "entertain serious apprehension in bringing to adjudication, before him, any cause of importance."[6] Lisle also served as Speaker of the Assembly and senior Assistant Justice of the Court of Common Pleas.

Musgrave, with his superior education, disdained the elected members of the House of Assembly, who were "neither in birth nor education respectable, as untutored as they are unprincipled" and among whom "there is not a single person whom I could consider as a fit associate for me." He preferred the company of the wealthier, appointed members of the Council, including Arthur Hodge. Declaring himself unable to determine "whatever may have been his conduct, previous to my arrival here," Musgrave was to describe him, based on the "nearly three years . . . I have been on terms of intimacy with Mr. Hodge," as "correct and honorable in his deportment, . . . a fond father, safe companion, and a candid and sincere friend."[7]

Among Hodge's other "bosom friends" identified by Musgrave was George Martin. Martin was a wealthy owner of three plantations and an Assistant Justice of Robertson's Court of Common Pleas. A bachelor, he had begun to produce a family of "spurious offspring"[8] by several of his mulatto slave women. Among these offspring was Kitty, born in 1810, to whom he was to leave a legacy of £5,000 sterling, and Abraham, born three years later, who was to inherit the bulk of his estate, including title to 639 slaves.[9] They fared better than Hodge's Bella.

Musgrave acted as counsel for Martin, as he had, before her death, for Mrs. Ruth Lettsom. As counsel for her family he procured for Martin appointment as "Guardian and Manager of the persons and estates of the children of the late Mrs. Ruth Lettsom." Martin soon used his position of manager of the largest estates on the island to increase his importance in the colony, indeed expecting all "to pay implicit homage to him."[10]

George Martin's brother–in–law was Henry Maurice Lisle, the

son of the Assembly Speaker and American agent. Henry Lisle had moved to Boston a dozen years before, where he had become an American citizen and a member of the Massachusetts bar. Now he returned to Tortola on a visit, considered the opportunities there and went back to get his wife. He soon established a practice in Tortola, obtaining appointments as a Justice of the Peace and Junior King's Counsel. Musgrave, who found Lisle to be of "despicable spirit," feared that Lisle yearned to replace him as attorney for the Lettsom estate and in the financially rewarding naval prize cases which came his way as Senior King's Counsel.[11]

Another actor in the drama that was about to unfold was William Cox Robertson. Robertson was a young man, a native of Tortola and the son of the widow Frances Pasea Robertson. Frances may have been widowed by one of Arthur Hodge's dueling pistols. In any case, she bore him a mortal hatred.

Young Robertson had been in England in 1809 and there had become deeply involved in debt. When Musgrave's younger brother and a group of friends bailed him out of debtor's prison, Robertson escaped to Tortola, leaving his sureties to cover his bail and rudely rejecting their demands for reimbursement. This behavior, and his treatment of his mother upon his return, soon caused him to be "despised and shunned by every worthy member of the community." Then, in what was said to be an attempt "to repair his shattered reputation by a display of personal valour," he responded to a remark by Arthur Hodge by challenging him, in a "scurrilous paper exhibited in the public streets," to a duel. Hodge consulted with Musgrave and other friends, who advised him not to accept the challenge since Robertson "had forfeited the character of a gentleman." Musgrave put his advice in writing and a war of words followed in which Robertson made serious charges against Hodge. Musgrave advised Hodge to bring a libel action against Robertson.

After the ensuing hearing, in September 1810, the Court of Sessions, which included Martin among its members, imposed fines upon all parties to the dispute, including Hodge and Musgrave. During the course of the proceedings Musgrave had argued to the

THE HANGING OF ARTHUR HODGE 103

court that there was a "fatal defect" in the proceedings in that it was "sitting without a legal adjournment." On this ground Musgrave and Hodge refused to pay their fines. Musgrave then sailed to Antigua and consulted the Attorney General of the Leeward Islands, John Burke, who agreed with his interpretation of the law. Musgrave had also planned to visit Hugh Elliot, the new Governor General, but was unable to do so because of Elliot's illness.

Upon his return to Tortola, the Grand Jury directed Musgrave to prosecute certain persons (just who it did not specify) for libeling Robertson. Musgrave argued to the court that this order put him in "a delicate situation" and Lisle, as Junior King's Counsel, was directed to proceed in his place. Nothing was done.

The tensions which had been building up in the community exploded on January 3, 1811, when George Martin invaded Hodge's house "and there most wantonly insulted and assaulted him." On the evening of the same day Martin "committed a similar outrage" upon Musgrave. Insulted by Martin's "gross and severe" expressions, considering the peace bond which the court had imposed on him in September invalid and believing "that the Law affords but a very inadequate reparation for insults," Musgrave felt compelled to resort to "the custom which prevails among men in certain situations in life as to the adjustment of private differences."

Musgrave sent his friend Dougan to demand of Martin the satisfaction of an apology. Martin refused to afford satisfaction or to meet Musgrave on the field of honor. Musgrave then determined that "there was nothing left for me but to render his cowardice as conspicuous as his insult to me," publicly proclaimed him a "coward" and, on the following day, January 10, had his opinion of Martin posted in several public places in Roadtown.

Shortly thereafter, on January 29, 1811, the House of Assembly adopted a petition to Governor Elliot in Antigua, asking that Musgrave be removed from "the high and important Situation of King's Counsel," and blaming him for much of the recent public strife during which "the lower class of people are daily committing the most flagrant, violent, and daring outrages against the peace by presenting Pistols, and other Weapons against the Constables, in the Execution of their duty, openly declaring that the Laws have no power over them."[12]

The petition was introduced in the Assembly by William Cox Robertson, with the support of Maurice Lisle and Henry Lisle. The Council, in which Arthur Hodge was the senior member after President Thomas Thomasson, refused to concur in it.

Musgrave replied to the Assembly in a long letter which he sent to Elliot the next day, questioning whether his "situation" was as important as the Assembly thought and stating that "the treatment which I have met with in Tortola but ill accords with the ideas which the House of Assembly affect to entertain of the dignity and importance of my office." After replying to each of the charges made against him in the petition, he closed by offering Elliot the hospitality of his home if he should have occasion to visit Tortola.[13]

Arthur Hodge had made his will in December. The bulk of his estate was to go to his son, Henry Cecil Hodge, when the boy reached the age of twenty–one, with individual legacies for each of the daughters. William Musgrave, Dr. William West and Thomas Dougan were named as trustees, with the education of the children being entrusted to James Hoggins, their uncle, of St. James College, Cambridge.[14]

Dr. William West, who witnessed the will together with his brother John and Richard Musgrave, the younger brother of the King's Counsel, was to receive Hodge's gold watch, swords and daggers. Dr. West's wife was given possession of Hodge's mistress Peggy and their much–abused daughter Bella, with the condition that should Mrs. West leave the West Indies the two slaves were to be set free.

Dr. John West and Thomas Dougan were each to receive a brace of pistols.[15]

Martin, enjoying his wealth and his mulatto mistresses, had not been prepared to risk his life in response to Musgrave's challenge but had instead sought a way, by destroying his livelihood, to force Musgrave from the island. Musgrave had never fought a duel, while Hodge had gained an "unenviable notoriety as a duelist."[16]   Now Martin learned that Hodge had made "half–uttered threats of calling (him) out."[17]   And while Martin was "by no means deficient in courage [he] thought it better not to fight him, without first attempting to deliver himself from such a desperate enemy, by bringing him to public justice."[18]

10

The Governor: "The Course of Duty"

Martin's fears soon became the concern of Hugh Elliot, the new British governor, to whom the House of Assembly had recently addressed its petition for the removal of William Musgrave. Elliot, who bore the impressive title of "Captain General and Governor in Chief in and over His Majesty's Leeward Charibee Islands in America, Chancellor, Vice Admiral and Ordinary of the Same," had arrived in Antigua to assume his duties a few months before, in July 1810. He had had a distinguished career as a British diplomat in Europe, but had not served in the colonies before.[1]

Now almost fifty–nine years of age, he had been born at Minto House, the family seat in Roxburghshire, Scotland, the son of Sir Gilbert Elliot, third baronet of Minto and for many years a member of Parliament. Sir Gilbert had been a close friend and supporter of King George III and a parliamentary advocate of his American policy. He had also established a reputation as a philosopher and song writer.

Hugh's brother Gilbert—the elder by less than a year—had been Governor–General of India since 1807 and now, in the winter of 1811, was leading his army in the conquest of Java.[2] Previously he had served in Parliament for over fifteen years, where in 1792 he had voted in favor of Wilberforce's motion for the immediate abolition of the slave trade.[3] Their brother–in–law, Lord Auckland, had carried the abolition bill in the Lords when it finally passed in 1807.[4]

Hugh Elliot

Hugh and Gilbert had been educated together, first by a private tutor and later, from 1764 to 1766, in Paris, where they were under the care of the Scottish philosopher and historian, David Hume. There, at the Pension Militaire, Hugh formed a lasting friendship with Mirabeau, the future leader of the revolutionary National Assembly. The Elliot brothers entered Oxford together in 1768.

Two years later, at the age of eighteen, Hugh returned to the continent to complete his military education at Metz. Soon he was fighting as an officer in the Russian army, then campaigning against the Turks in the Balkans. As a result of his exploits—including swimming the Danube while holding the tail of a Cossack's horse—he returned to London with the reputation of a "macaroni"—a young dandy who had been to the continent and returned to stick a feather in his cap and with the girls be handy.

When but twenty–one he secured, through his father's influence, an appointment as British Minister Plenipotentiary to Bavaria. Four years later he was named British ambassador to the court of Frederick the Great of Prussia. In Berlin he established the reputation for wit and quick repartee which he ever afterward enjoyed, while at the same time working hard to defeat the mission of the American envoys; going so far, it was said, as to arrange for the theft of their dispatch box and the copying of its contents.

In Berlin he wed for the first time. His German wife was unfaithful. Elliot challenged her lover to a duel in which he himself was wounded but received the satisfaction of a written apology. A short time later the Elliots were divorced. The scandal was to haunt him throughout his career and probably explains why he never earned a knighthood or bore a title.

Elliot then served in Copenhagen for seven years, during which time he gained fame for single-handedly stopping a war between Denmark and Sweden and restoring the King of Sweden to his throne.

In 1789, as the French Revolution was beginning the destruction of the old European order, he was back in London, soon to be sent on a secret mission to his old school friend Mirabeau, now the leader of the National Assembly.

In 1792 Elliot was named British ambassador to the court of Saxony in Dresden. Shortly before, nearly forty years of age, he had married his second wife Margaret, "a lovely girl . . . of humble origin,"[5] twenty years his junior. Their marriage was to be blessed by love, happiness and eleven children, all of whom—remarkably in that time—lived to adulthood.[6] His family was ever after to be his great joy and his great concern.

From Dresden the Elliots were sent to Naples, the capital of the Kingdom of the Two Sicilies. Elliot survived as ambassador to that tempestuous court—with its incompetent king and conniving queen (a sister of the guillotined Marie Antoinette), its English prime minister, French royalist war minister and Russian allies—from 1803 until Napoleon's occupation of the mainland provinces, the flight of the king and queen from Naples to Sicily and a change of ministries in London were followed by his recall in 1806.

Elliot was not to receive another appointment until 1809.[7] The intervening period was one of some economic pain for a middle–aged man with a large and growing family. But the recalled diplomat had yet another career ahead of him as a distinguished colonial administrator.

Upon the death of Lord Lavington Elliot was named to succeed him as Governor of the five presidencies which made up the Leeward Islands. Leaving his family in England from fear of the West Indian climate which had taken its toll of so many young Englishmen, Elliot traveled to Antigua with his private secretary and close family friend, Philip Heydinger.[8]

His first duty and desire was to visit each capital of his government to present the commission of office which made him governor, judge and bishop and to await with eagerness the vote of its separate legislature determining the amount of his salary. On August 2, 1810, he addressed the Council and Assembly of Antigua in St. John's.[9] In his address he questioned whether the existing form of government in the Leeward Islands was "defective" and promised to consider measures for remedying its defects. He then referred to the recent conquest of the French islands—as a result of which "not one harbour, not one solitary creek has been left, from which your security may be endangered"—and, putting on his ecclesiastical hat, urged the legislature to support the clergy and rights of the established Church. The newly arrived official made no mention of slavery.[9]

The Council and Assembly responded by voting their new Governor a salary of £1,500 sterling a year, an increase over that which had been granted to Lord Lavington.

At the end of the month Elliot, Heydinger, and their servants sailed to Montserrat. Heydinger, in a letter to Elliot's daughter Harriet, described the ceremonies in which the governor, the local president, the Council and the Assembly all pledged support to each other and to their "beloved sovereign" as a "swearing match."[10] By September 9 it was over, the salary had been voted and the party sailed on to the recently conquered island of Guadeloupe to meet with Admiral Sir Alexander Cochrane, who had been appointed Governor of the former French possession.[11]

A few days later they returned to Antigua where, being informed that the Powder Officer, "who has charge of all the Powder belonging to the Island and collects the Powder duty from all the Ships that arrive," had died, Elliot appointed Heydinger to the post, which was worth £300 a year.[12]

As September wore on Elliot's health gradually declined and on October 5 he fell seriously ill, suffering from a boil, fever, stomach distress and general weakness.

Not until mid–December was he well enough to write to his wife, expressing his thanks to Providence for his recovery.[13] He was not alone is his illness. The frigate *Perlen*, based at English Harbour, had lost eighty of her men in two months' time. Although this year had not been particularly sickly, yet among the troops stationed in Guadeloupe "different Regiments have buried the greatest portion of their men, and sickness and death have not been confined to the military, but have pervaded all classes of Society." He continued with his tale of disease and death, telling Margaret that

"I hope it may disgust any of my children from *soliciting* to be sent out upon service to the West Indies. If in the course of their duty they must come, may God preserve them, they may perhaps escape an untimely grave, but they may pay their account with being subject to fevers of the most fatal kind, which often leave the constitution broken for life, even if they do not prove mortal."

He went on to discuss his financial woes, telling his wife,

"My anxiety about your situation daily increases, and makes me miserable. It can be relieved *only by money*. . . . Antigua alone has paid me, from the other Islands I have not received one Shilling, neither do I expect to do so until I go to them. Perhaps with time and perseverance I might be able to pay my expences if the Islands pay me; but the outset has been dreadful."[14]

In an earlier letter he had worried about the cost of his white servants, who he would be rid of, "not that I have any complaint to make of them, but on account of their expence, of their little real utility and because the Black servants appear to me better in every respect and very much like the Italians."[15]

Later he was to complain that "there is rather a dirty and in-triguing spirit existing against me at Antigua in most of the late lord Lavington's friends, whose pompous manner, titles and string [of horses] have left a deep impression upon the vulgar minds of his favorites."[16]

In November, while ill, Elliot had received a request from the Earl of Liverpool, the Colonial Secretary and future Prime Minis-ter, for information concerning the case of "an opulent Planter in the Island of Nevis, named Huggins" whose cruelties toward his slaves had reached the ears of the authorities in London.[17] Elliot replied, sending Liverpool such papers as he had already collected

on the matter and promising to conduct a thorough investigation.
In his reply he diagnosed the reasons for the decline in government in the Leeward Islands, in language which, when printed by
order of the House of Commons, was to create a sensation in the
West Indies:

> "The fact is, the governments of the smaller islands were
> formed in times when many of the proprietors lived upon
> their estates, and the white population was, in some in-
> stances, perhaps ten times as numerous as it now is. Of the
> few white inhabitants who remain, managers, overseers, self–
> created lawyers, self–educated physicians, and adventurous
> merchants, with little real capital and scanty credit, compose
> the greatest part. The acquirements of education, among
> many of this description of persons, are very unequal to the
> task of taking a share in the governments. The prevalence of
> principle, either moral or religious, is also, I fear, not to be
> fairly calculated from the repetition of the hacknied expres-
> sions, of which an ostentatious use is frequently made in
> addresses, and on all occasions meant to meet the public eye
> at home.
>
> "To collect from such a state of society, men fit to be
> legislators, judges, or jurymen, is perfectly impracticable.
> Individual interest—personal influence—animosity of party
> feuds, weigh down the scale of Justice, and divert the course
> of legislative authority into acts of arbitrary and unjustifi-
> able power, cloaked under the semblance, and dignified
> with the name, of constitutional acts."[18]

The subject of Lord Liverpool's inquiry, Edward Huggins, Sr.,
had acquired such a reputation for cruelty on the island of Nevis
that, in the words of one of his accusers, "his conduct (is) held in
abhorrence by every good man in the community. Ignorant and
brutal as he is, he has amassed an immense fortune, and still is
grasping at the possession of more land and more Negroes. His

THE HANGING OF ARTHUR HODGE

doctrine was, that it was cheaper to buy Negroes than to breed them."[19]

A specific provision of the Leeward Islands Melioration Act forbade requiring slaves to carry dung, for fertilizer, to the fields during the hours after nightfall which were allowed them for private life and exhausted sleep.[20] Beset by a series of cruelties, Huggins' slaves finally refused this labor. On January 23, 1810, before Elliot had left England, in response to this refusal, Huggins marched thirty–two of them to the public market place in Charlestown, the island capital. There, in broad daylight, he and his sons set two drivers to whipping each of them; one from the left and one from the right, using whips with iron lashes at their tips. A visitor to the neighboring gallery of Dr. Crosse was amazed when the flogging of the first victim, Yellow Quashy, lasted for fifteen minutes or more and "under the impression that the country would take up the business," counted the lashes given to the other Negroes. One man received 242 lashes; another 212. A woman likewise received 212 and another woman 291. It was estimated that Yellow Quashy had received 365. One of the women was pregnant. An observer saw one of the men, "after he was whipped severely, scrape the blood from his buttocks and drink it."[21]

As the floggings continued the local gentry—intrigued or shocked—gathered in the market place or at Dr. Crosse's. Among them were several of the local magistrates, who had authority to interfere but who—ignorant of their authority, indifferent or frightened—failed to do so.

A week later the Nevis Assembly passed a resolution condemning Huggins and a week after that the *St. Christopher Gazette* printed a copy of the resolution. An indictment was obtained against Huggins, although he was never arrested or confined. On the first of May he came to trial. The Deputy Provost Marshal, who was responsible for the selection of the jury, produced two packs of cards. "One of them was put aside, and from the other, which was never shuffled or cut before the court, the Marshal drew the cards that were uppermost." A bystander observed to Samuel Long, one of Huggins' counsel, that "there are ten for Mr. Huggins and two against him." Long replied, "They should not have been there if I had known it."[22]

The jury acquitted Huggins.

Thomas Howe, the printer of the *St. Christopher Gazette*, was prosecuted for libel for having printed the resolution of the House of Assembly and was fined £25.

Elliot's recovery was slow, and it was not until February that he was able to resume his travels. On the 21st he wrote to Lord Liverpool from St. Christopher, reporting with satisfaction that the legislature had voted him the same increase in salary to £1,500 a year that had previously been granted by Antigua.[23]

Three days later he sailed on *H.M.S. Cygnet*, the frigate which was at his command, to Nevis. In his address to the Council and Assembly of that island he dwelt at length on the Huggins incident which, he declared, had "created painful sensations, not only within this island and the adjacent regions, but even in the breasts of His Majesty's Ministers, and of the inhabitants of the Metropolis of the British Empire." He urged the legislature to reform the island's Penal Code by limiting to thirty–nine the number of strokes which could be inflicted as punishment in order to avoid "the varying tempers, feelings, and mistaken judgment of individuals."[24]

On March 11 he returned to Antigua. There, on the 23rd, he received word that a delegation had arrived from the Virgin Islands and was anxious to see him.[25]

11

Hodge Arrested and Defended:
"Than To Kill His Dog"

The mission of the Virgin Islanders had its origins three weeks before. Alarmed by Hodge's "half–uttered threats" and Musgrave's challenge, George Martin had determined to eliminate his enemies, thinking "it a safer proceeding to hang his enemy than to fight him."[1] Charges were brought against Musgrave in the Court of Sessions, which met in March, growing out of Musgrave's challenge to Martin and his subsequent "libel." Musgrave believed that Martin's purpose was "to effect my ruin in this island" and he "determined to quit Tortola."[2] Regarding Hodge, Martin's purpose was more sinister.

On March 4 William Cox Robertson penned a note to Henry Maurice Lisle, the Junior King's Counsel, William Gumbs Chalwill and William Rogers Isaacs, all of whom were Justices of the Peace:

> "Gentlemen,
> "I have received information of a highly important nature. I
> request you will accompany me to a place, where I think it
> necessary a deposition should be taken."[3]

About dusk that same day a party of eight men, including the three justices, George Martin and Daniel Ross, rode up to the cabin of Penelope Hodge, an aged black woman who lived, with her husband, on the estate of Richard Hetherington, near that of

Arthur Hodge.[4] Henry Lisle administered an oath to the old woman and began to question her.

"Had Mr. Hodge ever murdered any of his negroes to her knowledge?"

"No. That she had never heard of any such thing. She had heard that Mr. Hodge had flogged some of this negroes, but she had seen them at their work afterwards."

Daniel Ross took over, asking how Bennery died and "whether he had not died from a whipping?"

She replied, "No—That she knew he had been flogged for stealing a tongue, but she saw him after the flogging at his work— and that she never heard nor knew of any negroes having died from flogging or severity."

Then she was asked "whether a certain negro named Jupiter had not been burnt to death? and whether a negro woman called Margaret had not been made by Mr. Hodge to drink hot or melted lead?"

The old woman replied, "Never, to her knowledge."

She did not know how Sarah, or Beck, or Tower Hill had died or "by whom the negro belonging to Mr. Wallace was lately shot."

She was questioned about the death of Mrs. Hodge and the miscarriage and death of Mrs. Hodge's white maid. Finally one of her interrogators said, "We can get nothing out of her; we must take her to town."

Then she was asked, "Where a woman called Perreen Georges was?" A little later Penelope saw Perreen with the men and overheard one of them tell her that she must go to Robert Green's house.

Perreen Georges' deposition was taken before George Martin, Daniel Ross and the three justices to whom William Cox Robertson had written earlier in the day.[5] In it she described the deaths, three and four years before, of Tom Boiler, Prosper, Cuffy, Tamson, Margaret and Elsey, signing the document with her mark.

Abraham Long, a planter and one of Martin's estate managers, left Tortola for St. Croix to find Stephen McKeough and persuade him to return.[6]

The next day William Cox Robertson swore before the magistrates that he "hath probable cause to suspect, and doth suspect that the Hon. Arthur Hodge of said Island of Tortola hath wilfully, feloniously and of his malice aforethought murdered the following negro slaves, late his property, to wit: Tom Boiler, Prosper, Cuffy, Margaret and Elsey. . .." He entered into a bond for £1,000 to appear at the next sitting of the Court of Sessions and prosecute his complaint.[7] The Deputy Provost Marshal was ordered to apprehend Hodge and bring him before the court.[8]

Hodge's party was also active. Thomas Dougan located Penelope Hodge and obtained a statement from her concerning the visit she had received the evening before.[9]

McKeough returned from St. Croix with Long and, together with Perreen, was lodged with Robert Green, who had managed the Bellevue estate before Hodge's return from England. They were under his protection, Green said, "as they were afraid of being assassinated, not by Mr. Hodge, but by his friends."[10]

McKeough's deposition was taken on March 10.[11] George Martin and Henry Lisle were both present. McKeough recounted the deaths of Welcome, Margaret and Elsey, Jupiter, Tom, Little Simon, Peter and others. He told of the mistreatment of Bella and the other children. McKeough closed by telling how Arthur Hodge had had his slaves steal tiles from a neighboring estate which belonged to the Bazaliel Hodge heirs, including Ruth Lettsom, and how he had used cattle from that estate to cart sugar from Bellevue down to the bay. McKeough had once been sent to bring the watchman in charge of the cattle to Arthur Hodge, bound. Hodge threatened to cartwhip the watchman if he told anyone of Hodge's use of the cattle. The watchman, upon agreeing to keep the secret, had been rewarded with corn, meal and herrings.

Five days later Martin took another deposition from McKeough.[12] This time he told of the deaths of Violet and her son, and of Dick, who had stolen a goose.

Perreen Georges went with members of the "committee for carrying on the prosecution," including doctors, to the Hodge estate and pointed out the site of Prosper's grave.[13] It was opened and the bones exhumed, as were those of others, who had been buried in their chains.[14]

On March 12 President Thomas Thomasson signed a proclamation offering a reward of 400 joes, or 3,200 Spanish dollars, which had been authorized by the Council and Assembly, for the apprehension of Arthur Hodge, who, it was said, was being "harboured and secreted by some person or persons in the Virgin Islands."[15] Hodge then presented himself to the marshal and was committed to the jail in Roadtown. Once jailed he was chained.[16]

On the fifteenth a writ of habeas corpus was issued, directing William Bagnell, the marshal, to produce Hodge in court the next day.[17]

At the hearing on the writ William Musgrave urged the court to release his client on bail, boldly asserting the proposition that a negro, being property, "it was no greater offense in law for his owner to kill him, than it would be to kill his dog."[18]

The four sitting Justices of the Peace, who included Henry Lisle, ordered Hodge returned to jail. That same day, a Saturday, President Thomasson ordered George Porter, representing the Council, and Henry Lisle, from the Assembly, to Antigua with an introduction to Governor Elliot and instructions to consult with Attorney General John Burke.[19]

Porter and Lisle reached Antigua on the twenty–third and wrote to Elliot, acquainting him with the nature of their mission. They presented him with copies of the depositions of Perreen Georges and Stephen McKeough and asked that he direct counsel for the Crown to prepare indictments based on them and travel to Tortola to support those indictments.[20] Elliot met with them that day. Following the meeting he requested Burke to prepare the necessary indictments. When Porter and Lisle reminded Burke that the Court of Sessions would adjourn on April 3, not to sit again until September, Burke prepared the documents necessary for Elliot to call a special session of court at Roadtown so that the trial could proceed as expeditiously as possible. Since Burke's health was such that he could not travel, Elliot asked Paul Horsford, the Solicitor General, to travel to Roadtown to conduct the trial.[21]

Elliot also wrote to President Thomasson, noting that the jail at Roadtown as "in a very insecure state" and that two persons confined for murder had recently "eloped." He directed Thomasson to take "the most efficacious measures the law will admit of for the better securing" of Hodge and authorized him to request troops from the military authorities in the neighboring islands.[22]

On the first of April he wrote to Lord Liverpool concerning his recent activities. He had intended, while in Antigua, he wrote, to prepare a report on his recent trip to St. Christopher and Nevis. The arrival of Porter and Lisle from the Virgin Islands had prevented that. "Great indeed," he declared, "is my mortification in being prevented from accomplishing this object by an incident more black and atrocious (according to the representations of it made to me), than any previous example of oppression, tyranny, and cruelty which has hitherto appeared in the annals of British History." He looked at what he had written, considered it and crossed out "appeared," substituting "disgraced." Again he thought, and replaced "disgraced" with "stained." Finally he wrote, " . . . which has hitherto polluted the annals of British History." He had acted, he advised Liverpool, to suspend Hodge from his position as the member of the Council second in seniority to President Thomasson.[23]

About ten days before Musgrave had been brought to trial on a charge of having breached the peace by issuing his challenge to George Martin. He had been convicted and fined £50.

On Monday, April 1, with the Court of Sessions scheduled to adjourn on Wednesday, he was tried again—this time for having libeled Martin by accusing him of cowardice after he refused Musgrave's challenge. After his jury had deliberated for eighteen hours, they returned with a verdict of guilty. This time Musgrave was fined £200 and ordered to prison for two months.

A Portion of Elliot's Draft of His Dispatch of April 1, 1811, to
Lord Liverpool - Courtesy of the Trustees of the National
Library of Scotland

The next day he wrote to Governor Elliot, asking for a pardon
and offering to resign his position as King's Counsel and leave
Tortola, where "Mr. Martin appears to be bent on my destruction." In asking for his pardon, Musgrave mentioned several admiralty cases which he had ready for trial for the Navy and the fact
that "I am also employed as counsel for Mr. Hodge in the prosecution about to be instituted against him."

Summarizing Musgrave's letter in a dispatch to Liverpool, Elliot
wrote, "Mr. Musgrave considers the accusations against Arthur
Hodge as the result of a foul conspiracy, and has communicated to
the counsel proceeding from hence affidavits in support of that
assertion." He continued, "My duty is to see justice done to all
parties, and it is upon this principle I have released Mr. Musgrave

from confinement, in order that he may have an opportunity of exerting his professional abilities in favour of his client."[24]

While this was going on the evidence which had been solicited against Hodge was being withheld from his counsel from fear, Henry Lisle was later to state, that "if the prisoner or his friends were permitted to know who had testified against him they might never be forthcoming."[25]

On the second Elliot sailed on the *Cygnet* to St. Kitts, where he executed the commissions for the extraordinary session of a Court of Oyer and Terminer and Gaol Delivery in Tortola.[26] Heydinger followed a few days later.

From St. Kitts Heydinger wrote to Elliot's daughter Harriet on the 17th that

> "In about four days we shall proceed to Tortola—which will be the last place where the ceremony of opening the Commission and the swearing match are to be performed. I suppose we shall remain there near three weeks and perhaps the Governor may visit some of the neighboring islands before he returns here."[27]

Governor Elliot wrote to his wife Margaret on the same day, giving more detail concerning the planned trip to Tortola,

> "On the 20th of this month," he told her, "I am to leave St. Christophers in H.M.S. Cygnet, to go to Tortola, where I am in the first place, as usual, to open my Commission, etc.—but where I am afterwards to witness a most painful scene. A considerable planter in that island, named Arthur Hodge, Esq., a member of the Council and a Gentleman well known in England, and connected by marriage to families of distinction there, father of a family, has been thrown into prison upon the accusation of having *murdered many of his slaves* by severe punishments and various kinds of torture. His trial is to take place on the 25th inst. and Mr.

Horsford, the Solicitor General in this Government goes with me in the Cygnet as the principal Lawyer to conduct the prosecution against Mr. Hodge. The eyes of all the West Indies are turned towards this cause and it will create a no less general sensation in Great Britain. My business is to see justice impartially distributed and that the proceedings shall meet with no interruption nor be disgraced by any irregularity on either side. The enormities laid to the charge of this Mr. Hodge by his accusers are more dreadful that any I have ever heard of within the limits of the British Empire. On the other hand, his defenders assert that the accusation is founded in a foul conspiracy to deprive the prisoner of his life and honor. In the meantime the state of party at Tortola is represented to be violent and inflamed, and the island is, in fact, without any regular force whatever which can act upon an emergency for the support of the civil power or of tranquility. The law must take its course in this disagreeable business—God grant that it may be directed to its proper object—that the guilty may suffer and the innocent escape."[28]

12

Trial: "This Case—For The Honor Of The World—Has No Parallel"[1]

Preparation

Solicitor General Paul Horsford, accompanied by George Tyson, the Speaker of St. Kitts, and Samuel Long, who had defended Edward Huggins, sailed for Tortola on April 20. Tyson and Long were to assist Musgrave in defending Hodge.[2] Henry Maurice Lisle, Junior King's Counsel, formerly of Boston, recently elected member of the Assembly of the Virgin Islands, was to be Horsford's co–counsel.[3]

The *Cygnet* sailed again from St. Christophers on the evening of April 25, to the accompaniment of a nineteen gun salute,[4] bearing Elliot, Heydinger and the Reverend John Julius Kerie, rector of the parishes of Saint Anne Sandy Point and Saint Paul Capisterre, whom Elliot brought with him "purposely to attend the prisoner in case of condemnation."[5] The Reverend Kerie had committed his life to presiding over services in half–empty chapels and bringing the gospel of Jesus Christ to a community based on slavery. He must have had an opportunity to talk over dinner with Hugh Elliot, the representative in the Leeward Islands of the head of Christ's church on earth—His Majesty, King George III, who had just lost his sanity for the last time. Elliot, in his youth, had been a close friend of George, Prince of Wales, whom Parliament had named as

Prince Regent in January. Elliot was greatly troubled by the King's failing health.[6]

Philip Heydinger probably did not enjoy the passage. He had just written to Harriet Elliot concerning her father that "I am always happy to escape being at sea with him—for there he imagines himself the only person who can do anything right, or keep out of danger, and generally contrives to be a great plague to me."[7]

The next day was cloudy, windy, and rainy—with the moist, warm Caribbean wind which sends bits of black clouds scudding across the gray sky. From Roadtown, Tortola, Heydinger reported,

> "We . . . arrived here about noon today. The place seems miserable enough—there is but one long street, which constitutes the town, and the whole country is mountainous. We are lodged in a very good house, belonging to a Mr. Hill, about a mile from town—and nearer Heaven than ever I lived before."[8]

Captain Russell of the *Cygnet* began a new log book on Sunday, April 28. Someone may have taken the old one of the jail to obtain the autograph of the Virgin Islands' most famous resident for below the entry for Saturday, the 27th, is the signature: "A. W. Hodge."[9]

Elliot's commission for a Special Court of Oyer and Terminer and Gaol Delivery had been ceremonially opened in Roadtown on April 9 and the court had then been adjourned to Thursday, April 25. At that day's session Hodge, in the custody of Robert Isaacs, the marshal, was brought to the bar. The Grand Jury presented an indictment charging him with the murder of Prosper in violation of both the common law and the Melioration Act. Other indictments had also been prepared.

*Log of H.M.S. Cygnet for April 27, 1811, bearing
signature of A. W. Hodge*

Hodge was asked "in what manner he would be acquitted" of
the indictment. He responded that he was not guilty and that
"concerning this for good and ill (he) puts himself upon his Country." He then asked that Long, Tyson and Musgrave be recognized
as his counsel.[10] (It was later reported that he paid them £900
sterling to conduct his defense).[11]

Tyson rose to advise the court that he was not ready for trial.
Horsford interposed, on behalf of the Crown, suggesting that only
one of the several attorneys for the defense should be allowed to
address the jury. Chief Justice Robertson, who was presiding,
rejected Horsford's suggestion, saying that he had sat for twenty–
four years and "never knew that counsel in the fullest extent

was refused in crimes of less degree . . . he should be sorry to sit where a prisoner was debarred counsel in the fullest extent." It was finally agreed that two of the prisoner's counsel could address the jury but that only one could examine or cross–examine any particular witness.

Tyson then claimed to have been surprised by the depositions or written statements which had been taken from McKeough and Perreen Georges. Moreover, he said, the defense team had expected to proceed to trial for the deaths of the first slaves mentioned in the depositions, Welcome and Tom Boiler. They had not prepared a defense to the charges involving Prosper. Long joined in, wanting to know why the depositions had been kept from them. The defense had thus been deprived of an opportunity of questioning the character of the witnesses, who were facing the defendant for the first time. Musgrave pointed out that the depositions had never been read to Hodge.

Lisle, admitted, for the Crown, that the depositions had been "kept back because if the prisoner or his friends were permitted to know who had testified against him, they might never be forthcoming."

An affidavit was then submitted on behalf of Hodge, stating that he was not prepared to proceed and asking to have the trial put off until the following Monday, the 29th of April. The court unanimously agreed. Lisle asked if the depositions should be lodged with the court. Long interjected to ask what the purpose would be if the prisoner's counsel could not see them. The court directed that the depositions be filed and said that it would allow the counsel for Hodge to read them, but not to make copies.[12]

Monday, the 29th, broke cloudy and breezy, with squalls rising by noon.[13] The court convened at 10:00 A.M. Seated on the bench were five members of the Council, Chief Justice Robertson and five other members of the Court of Common Pleas. After an argument about the form of the indictment, Hodge was brought in and repeated his plea of "not guilty." The next order of business was the selection of a jury.[14] A panel of thirty–nine white males was presented. The selection process began.

The first member of the panel presented for examination by the defense counsel was Robert Green, Hodge's former manager. Samuel Long questioned him.

"Was not Mr. McKeough entertained by you at the cost of the prosecution?"

"Mr. McKeough has been entertained at my house. He still eats and drinks with me, as does Perreen Georges, both at my own charge."

"Have you had any conversations with the witnesses?"

"I have, and wish to be excused; though I can conscientiously go upon the panel and do my duty towards Mr. Hodge and the King."

Horsford and Henry Lisle, for the Crown, argued that Green should be seated, since he had declared that his conversations with the witnesses had "made no bias on his mind." Tyson replied, "That man knows little of the human heart, who does not know what impressions such conversations would have. First impressions are the strongest—the law says we won't run the risk of the man being perjured."

Green was dismissed. Four peremptory challenges and one with cause followed before Long questioned Robert Bowie.

"Do you bear any ill will towards Mr. Hodge?"

"None. I have had a dispute with him."

"Have you conversed with the witnesses?"

"No."

Bowie was seated, the first juror.

More challenges followed, until the prisoner's counsel had peremptorily challenged nineteen of the veniremen.

Horsford then began his questioning. George Fisher was dismissed since, he admitted, being a third cousin he was prejudiced in favor of the prisoner.

Andrew Dougan was called.

Horsford asked, "Have you ever conversed with the prisoner on the subject of this trial, and when?"

"I have twice—have visited him in jail, and am prejudiced in his favor."

He was dismissed, as was John Rawbone, the husband of Hodge's sister Ann.

William Palmer was the eleventh member of the jury to be seated. Horsford had asked him, "Have you expressed any opinion on this case?" To which Palmer had replied, "I have spoken feelingly on it; I am not prejudiced."

John McDonough was then called and, before the questioning began, expressed his opinion that "the case will be hurtful to the West–India Islands; it would make the negroes saucy."[15]

Horsford said he was astonished at such a declaration and left it to the court whether McDonough should be admitted to the jury. Tyson replied that McDonough's opinion did not mean that the conviction or acquittal of Hodge would make the negroes saucy; the mere fact of the trial itself would do that. He ought therefore to be seated. The court disagreed.

Finally John Brubey was admitted and the jury was complete.

Stephen McKeough and Perreen Georges were ordered separated from the other witnesses and the indictment was then read to the jury.

Courtroom in Tortola

Prosecution[16]

Henry Lisle now rose to make the opening statement on behalf of the Crown. He began his speech, which was to last for more than three hours, by referring to the seriousness of the charges and the importance of the right to trial by jury. Then he turned to the situation of the prisoner.

"When we reflect, gentlemen of the jury, for a moment, that the unfortunate prisoner at the bar was born to, and did inherit a clear and ample estate, that he was rocked in the cradle of ease and nursed on the lap of affluence; that he received not only a liberal, but polished, education; that independence, with all her train, bearing concomitant blessings, attended him, that his prospects were once fair as could have been coveted; that the goddess, Fortune, was his handmaid; that honors awaited him, and his Sovereign called him in early life to his Council—we cannot but now look with wonder at his degradation, and pity the deplorable state to which his barbarous criminality has reduced him."

But he advised the jury not to be swayed by pity, nor by the length of time since the crimes had been committed. Then, growing dramatic, Lisle compared Hodge to Macbeth and, alluding to the dagger which he kept at the head of his bed, imagined that "The spectre of the murdered being flits before him—betwixt heaven and him, congealing him with fear and palsying the arm which would otherwise grasp the stiletto at the head of his bed, were not the former rendered nerveless and the latter innoxious to the gliding phantom."

The prosecutor then presented the jury with a lengthy description of the elements of the crime of murder, explaining the necessity for premeditation or malice. "What but malice," he asked, "induced that monster in cruelty to, coolly, lay down his miserable slave and cartwhip him for upwards of an hour at the works? What but malice, diabolical malice, could instigate him, after the poor helpless forlorn creature was lacerated till his flesh hung in shreds upon him, to order him up to the house of the gill, and there again, after having lashed him to a tree, a second time, to beat, cut, wound and torment the victim of his cruelty, until nature was exhausted, and his head fell down backwards, and he was not longer able to bawl? What but malice induced him to confine, chain, famish and persecute even until death the friendless African?" Bellevue Mountain, site of the Hodge estate, rose across the harbor outside the courtroom window. Pointing to it, Lisle continued, "Turn humanity, turn from the melancholy, dreadful spectacle, for 'tis one thou canst not bear to contemplate; turn from that fatal spot, that modern Golgotha, for every breeze that passes it is loaded with the groans of dying Africans, and every echo from yonder mountain reverberates nothing but murder! Turn and view the monster who has perpetrated those barbarous deeds, and execrate his cruelties, whilst justice awaking from her slumbers shall decide his fate."

"Prosper died," Lisle went on, "Prosper was murdered—murdered by the man to promote whose interests the strength of his youth was exhausted, to till whose fields his labors early and late had been devoted. Yes, by the man, by his own master, by him who ought to have protected him, soothed him, encouraged him and kindly supported him, was Prosper murdered; and notwithstanding the heinousness of the offence, the magnitude of the guilt, when the prisoner was brought up a few days since, under a writ of Habeas Corpus, it was not only asserted to be an offence bailable at law, but it was absolutely asserted—blush humanity, blush justice, to hear it—it was boldly asserted, that a negro, being property, 'it was no greater offence in law for his owner to kill him, than it would be to kill his dog.'

"My God! Are we patiently to hear such a declaration? Is this or any other community silently to permit it to be made, and not express its indignation? Forbid it Heaven—forbid it God Almighty!"

Lisle then explained to the jury the law regarding the rights of parents over their children and of masters over servants and that the prisoner could be found guilty although he had not wielded the whip himself.

"Gentlemen," he asked, "is it true that 'man is guilty of no greater offence in killing his negro than he would be in killing his dog?'" "No," he replied with quotations and examples, basing his conclusion both on the common law of England and on the Melioration Act.

Lisle then anticipated the defense by raising the question of conspiracy. "In order, gentlemen, to prejudice the minds of those, who from the community at large, might compose a jury of trial on this occasion, and to influence them in favor of the prisoner, it has been industriously and generally circulated by one or two, his friends and adherents that this prosecution is altogether the result of a conspiracy. . . .. This, gentlemen, is the last resort to detraction, to low cunning, and mean artifice, which that man, the prisoner at the bar (who has often boasted that he had a head to plan and an arm to execute) will ever practice.

"Who, gentlemen, are intended to be represented as conspirators? Who are characters thus vilified and slandered? Need I tell you? Who but your magistrates, who issued their warrant to apprehend this man of blood? Who but your representatives? The Commons House of Assembly of the Virgin Islands! The Honorable members of His Majesty's Council too are members of this conspiracy, and why? Truly, because the council and assembly of the Virgin Islands, hearing of the accusations against the prisoner, resolved that a prosecution should be carried on against him, the expense of which should be paid out of the public treasury, and on his absconding, on his fleeing from justice, the president himself became a conspirator, by issuing a proclamation, offering one hundred johannes for his apprehension and forbidding all persons to sustain, harbor or secrete him."

The magistrates and others, Lisle declared, had simply done their duty. The jury must now see and do its duty. "By whom accused, or from what motives Mr. Hodge has been arrested, are, gentlemen, questions immaterial to you. In order to investigate the charge against him, it is quite sufficient that he has in the due course of law been indicted, has pleaded and is now on trial.

"Why he was not sooner arrested and brought to trial you may as well, individually, ask yourselves, as any other person; for you must each, as well as the rest of the community, have learned from rumor the catalogue of his crimes, but what is everybody's business usually is performed by nobody, and not knowing where testimony might be procured of his guilt, no individual would risk the chance of rendering himself the victim of Mr. Hodge's resentment and vengeance by making accusations he might not be able to substantiate as true. For you well know, gentlemen, that only on the evidence of free persons can a free person be convicted. Policy has decreed that slaves shall only be permitted to testify against their fellow slaves, and not against free persons, in any case whatsoever. Were it otherwise, I would here introduce a number of sable wretches as witnesses bearing the external marks of the prisoner's cruelty, whose very appearance would make humanity shudder, and whose tales of woes would cause every nerve within you to vibrate with mental agony."

Then he closed by reminding the jurors of their oaths, their duty to their country, their King and their God and that for the verdict which they would give each would be accountable when he appeared "before the judgment seat of Jehovah."

Perreen Georges was then called to the witness stand. She was first examined on "voire dire," a process in which defense counsel were able to call into question the credibility of prosecution witnesses before their examination by counsel for the Crown.

Musgrave asked her, "Have you had any promise of reward from the persons who went out to take your deposition?"

She replied, "I have not. I was taken by the magistrates and only sworn to tell the truth."

"Were you ever persuaded to give testimony in this business?"

"Never. I have never been persuaded to come forward, nor has anybody ever held out any temptation or inducement to me."

Lisle then rose to object to Musgrave's line of questioning, declaring, "If it is the intention of the prisoner's counsel to accuse the magistrates of tampering with the witness, let them be impeached."

Samuel Long rose to his associate's defense. "If the counsel for the prisoner are stopped in this way, on a supposition, that it was their intention to incriminate the magistrates, which was not the case; if I have not the opportunity of acting as my judgment leads me for my client, I must abandon him. . . .. All I ask is to be heard in reason—my learned friend can oppose—if I am heard, and at large, I shall not complain."

The parties and the court quieted down, and Solicitor General Horsford began to question Perreen on behalf of the Crown.

"Do you know the prisoner at bar?"

"I do."

"Did you know a negro man slave, named Prosper, his property?"

"I know he owned a slave named Prosper."

"Is he dead?"

"He is."

"Do you know what occasioned his death?"

"He died by licks, confinement and starvation."

"By whose order was this done?"

"By order of Mr. Hodge—he was present."

"Were you present when the licks were inflicted?"

"I was present when he was laid down and flogged for a mango which dropped off a tree, and which Mr. Hodge said he should pay six shillings for. He had not the money, and came to borrow it of me. I had no more than three shillings. He said to his master he had no more money. His master said he would flog him if he did not bring it. He was laid down and held by four negroes on his face and belly and flogged with a cartwhip. He was under the lash better than an hour; he then got up to the hill after—and his master said he should be flogged again, if he did not bring the other three shillings. He was tied to a tree next day and the flogging was repeated. He was then licked so long that his head fell back and he could not bawl out any longer. I supposed he was faint. I then went from the window, as I could not bear to see any more of it."

Horsford asked, "Did Mr. Hodge call this kind of punishment by any particular name?"

"He did," she replied. "He called it short quarters."

"What do you mean by short quarters?"

"The whip is half tied up, and half let out."

"What was done with him after the second flogging?"

"He was carried to the sick house and put in irons."

"Was he flogged afterwards?"

"I did not see him flogged again."

"How long after did he die?"

"In about a week."

"Was he in irons all the time?"

"He was in chains with two other men for five days. They broke away, but he was so weak he could not go far."

"Where did he go?"

"From the sick house to his own house."

"Was he still in chains?"

"The other negroes loosed his chains."

"Was the prisoner," Horsford asked, indicating Hodge, "told of the negroes getting away."

"He was," Perreen replied.

"By whom?"

"By the driver."

"Was he informed about Prosper?"

"I do not know."

"Can you state how long it was, after the second flogging that he died?"

"It was not quite two weeks; it happened a little before Mrs. Hodge died."

"What was the cause of Prosper's death."

"He died by licking, confinement and starvation. He had no black skin upon him, he was all cut to rags."

"The whole body?"

"The back part of him—at the time he died crawlers were in him."

"Was he attended by a doctor."

"No doctor saw him."

"Did any doctor attend the estate?"

"Dr. West was the doctor of the estate, but I do not know if he was called to Prosper."

"Where was he buried?"

"Nearly on the spot he died. He was dragged to the door."

"Is there a burying ground on the estate?"

"There is."

"Do you know by whose order he was buried, and if in a coffin?"

"No person would take upon himself to do it without Mr. Hodge's orders. He was not buried in a coffin."

"In what state was the body?"

"It was spoiled and offensive, by which means I found it out."

"State again how long after the second flogging he died."

"In less than a fortnight."

A member of the jury was then given permission to question the witness, and asked, "Were you present during the whole of the time of the last flogging?"

Perreen responded, "I was. The first flogging was at the works and the second was on the hill."

Samuel Long then interjected and began his cross–examination by remarking, "Then I presume that Mr. Hodge made it a practice to have you present whenever he punished negroes."

Lisle objected. Long argued that on cross–examination he was not restricted to "any particular mode of examination" but could introduce new matter in an attempt to attack the credibility of the witness. Then he resumed his questioning of Perreen Georges.

"Were you present on the first day?"

"I was. It was at the works."

"Were you present on the second day?"

"I was. It was at the hill."

"How came you to be at the hill?"

"I was washing at the bottom, and brought up clothes to the hill."

Chief Justice Robertson then interposed a question, "Was or was not Mr. Hodge present when it began?"

Perreen replied, "He was at the beginning. He was present at both all the time."

Long took over again, "What did you mean by saying he was at the beginning?"

"He was there from beginning to end."

"Do you understand the nature of an oath, or the rules of religion?"

"I understand religion so far that I will tell the truth."

"How many lashes," Long asked, "do you think were given in the hour?"

"Better than one hundred," she answered. "Mr. Hodge has flogged for half an hour, for one hour and for two hours. He was tied and flogged them from breakfast until noon."

"Have you ever heard Mr. Hodge mention close quarters?"

"I have heard him mention close quarters."

"Have you ever heard Mr. Hodge to others mention the same?"

"No."

"Did you ever hear him mention it to his friends?"

"He did not do it to them."

"How long before Mrs. Hodge's death was Prosper flogged?"

"About three or four months."

"Did you stay there after this happened?"

"I remained working for Mrs. Hodge."

"Did you ever mention it to anyone?"

"I dared not."

"How long did you live there?"

"Until Mrs. Hodge died, and three or four weeks after."

One of the judges asked from the bench, "Were any persons besides the family there when this happened?"

"Nobody besides Mrs. Hodge and the children."

"Was not Mrs. Collins, now Mrs. Rawbone, there?"

Perreen replied, "She was not there that day."

Long resumed. "Did you ever mention Mr. Hodge's cruelty to anyone?"

"I mentioned it to slaves."

"Did you not mention it in town?"

"I did mention it in town."

"Did you never mention it to any free person?"

"I cannot recollect that I ever did."

"Were you not well disposed towards Mr. Hodge?"

"I could not like a man so cruel as Mr. Hodge."

"Did he not treat you well?"

"He was always very kind to me, but very cruel to his slaves."

"Have you always said so?"

"I have."

"Who did you ever speak to in this manner?" Long asked, looking for the name of a free person whom he could call to contradict her testimony.

Perreen replied, "I can't recollect that I ever said it to any free person."

Moving on to another subject, Long asked, "Where was Prosper taken after he was flogged?"

"He was carried to the sick house."

"Did not Dr. West attend the sick house?"

"I never saw him attend more than three people, and they were afflicted by the Lord."

"Were there many people at the sick house?"

"There were, and all cut up."

"Was the smell of the sick house offensive?"

"It was."

"Did not the doctor visit the sick house?"

"I do not know. The three people I mentioned were at the old manager's house."

"How is the sick house situated?"

"It is near the great house. People going there pass by it."

"Did not other people notice its being offensive?"

"Other people did not tell me it was offensive. I found it so myself."

"Have you ever observed that the negroes were lacerated, when they came from the field?"

"I have—so much so that they stunk."

"Do you know the cause of Prosper's death?"

"He died of the beating."

"Did it not occur to you that Mr. Hodge was guilty of a crime?"

"It did."

"Did you not think that the law would punish him?"

"I did."

"Why did you not bring him forward?"

"I dared not. Mr. Hodge would kill me dead."

"Did you remain on the estate after Mrs. Hodge died?"

"I stayed a little time."

"Were you permitted to see Mrs. Hodge?"

"Mr. Hodge would not let me take my work in to her."

"What did you do with it?"

"I took it away with me."

"Were you there when Mrs. Hodge died? How long did you stay after?"

"I was there when she died, and stayed a week or two after."

"Was McKeough there when she died?"

"Yes."

"Was McKeough there when Prosper was flogged?"

"I cannot say. He was not there when he died."

Long was still seeking for a contradiction which he could use to attack the witness's credibility.

"Did you live on the estate?"

"I used to do work for Mrs. Hodge. I lived in town and went there occasionally."

"Were you there when Prosper died?"

"No, but I saw him after he was dead."

"Was Mrs. Collins there?"

Horsford observed that the witness was speaking of an occurrence which had taken place three or four years before. To which Long replied, "This renders it more difficult to repel a charge of that distant date."

He continued, "Were you constantly on the estate?"

"I did not always stay there," Perreen replied. "It was not my home. I would stay sometimes two weeks, sometimes three days."

"Was Mrs. Collins there?" Long asked, referring again to Hodge's sister, Ann.

"I do not know though I lodged in the white people's house."

Then, searching for a new subject on which he might impeach the witness, Long asked, "Did you know Margaret and Elsey, and are they dead or alive?"

"Yes, I was there when both died."

Henry Lisle rose to address the court for the prosecution. "Mr. Long has asked questions which appear to have a general tendency. If it is the intention to treat the matter generally, the counsel for the Crown would be ready to meet him, but caution him how he proceeds."

Long replied to Lisle, "I am contented. I was only using the latitude allowed counsel in cross-examination." Then he turned again to Perreen.

"What was the matter with Margaret?"

"I saw her skull almost split open."

Long had started; he had to go on.

"Was anything the matter with Elsey?"

"She was confined in consequence of licks and by being scalded with boiling water."

"By whose order?"

"By Mr. Hodge's order."

"Were you there when Margaret died?"

"I was. She died in the sick house on Christmas day. I heard Mr. Hodge say he would be the death of Margaret and Elsey, because they had tried to destroy his children."

"Did Margaret die before or after Mrs. Hodge's death?"

"Before."

"Was Mrs. Collins there?"

"I do not know whether she was there or not."

"Was Mrs. Arrindell there?"

"She was."

"Did Mrs. Arrindell see her?"

"Margaret could not be seen by anyone, she was so cut up."

"Was she in chains?"

"When dying Mr. Hodge took her out of chains and shackles and she died in the sick house."

"Was she long sick?"

"She was sick some time."

"Did not Mrs. Arrindell know of Margaret's death?"

"She might have heard of her death, but she could not see her, as she could not be seen while Mrs. Arrindell was there—Margaret's feet were shackled."

Long finished and Henry Lisle began redirect examination on behalf of the Crown.

Lisle asked, "Was not Margaret the cook?"

"She was."

"Was she not in the kitchen the day preceding the night she died?"

"She was—on Christmas day when she was taken out of the sick house. She was chopping minced meat."

"Did you observe anything particular about her?"

"Yes. She looked stupid. She showed me her head. In the back part of it you could have put three fingers."

"Did she tell you whom this was done by?"

"She said it was done by Mr. Hodge."

"What happened afterwards?"

"She sat down and I did for her what she had to do. Her head was then dropping. I told her to go from thence. She said, 'I can't go from here as I am to be confined tonight.'"

"Did Mr. Hodge ask you any question respecting Margaret?"

"He did. He sent to call me, and asked if Margaret had told me anything. I said to him that she was getting the fever."

"Why did you say so?"

"Because I feared he would lick the people who told me. He already locked me up once in the sick house, on account of money he owed me. He owes me money now, and I have been afraid to ask for it."

"Why were you afraid to ask for it?"

"On account of personal danger. I was afraid to say what Margaret told me, and that she showed me her head."

Lisle then turned to the court, asking permission to present "general testimony as to Mr. Hodge's cruel disposition."

Long asked permission to re–examine Perreen Georges on the subject matter which had just been covered by Lisle.

Lisle turned to Perreen, asking, "What was the general treatment of Mr. Hodge to his slaves?"

Before she could answer Tyson was objecting, "The point of examination for the prosecution is to support particular facts. The question now at issue is the murder of Prosper. Was ever evidence allowed to be given of general character on a charge of murder? Would they attempt to prove that Mr. Hodge was guilty of twenty murders on a trial for only one?

"If it appears that we can prove false swearing with regard to Margaret and Elsey, the jury will not credit the witness and our object in cross–questioning was to establish this false swearing, and we are clearly able to support this assertion. We shall affect her credit—indeed, invalidate her testimony. Suppose a witness is so completely drilled that you cannot detect her on the case immediately before the court; are we to be debarred endeavouring to prove she has committed improper acts, even in other cases, to answer this purpose?

"The object of the King's Counsel is to blacken the character of the unfortunate gentleman at the bar, and, in the event of their failing in this prosecution, they would tell the jury, 'It is true he is not guilty of this murder, but you have it in evidence that he has committed others, and you must consequently find him guilty of murder.' I submit that the court cannot permit them to enter into such examination."

Solicitor General Horsford replied, "We have particularly confined ourselves in examining this witness to the charges laid in the indictment. My learned friends have traveled out of it, by examining as to particular cruelties to particular objects. Having laid in the indictment that the prisoner at the bar was a person 'of a cruel, malicious and diabolical disposition' we have a right to enter into it. It will not help out our indictment but as it regards Prosper, therefore the examination we have entered into is only to guard the witness against the traps laid for her.

"If it is proved that Mr. Hodge was a saint, it will not avail him, if he is proved to have murdered Prosper. His counsel were warned, and we have a right, if they open a door, to enter it. We don't mean to support our charge by showing the general bad character of the prisoner, we only support the witness, who, as yet, is unimpeached."

"It appears to me," the Chief Justice observed, "that it would be time to support the witness when she is contradicted."

Counsel for the prosecution were given leave to continue.

By this time the afternoon must have been well along and the jury asked to be permitted to retire to refresh themselves. When they returned Lisle began the questioning again.

"What happened to Margaret after she nodded?"

"She was sitting down and appeared to be dying. She had a wound on the back of her head. She fell on her face, was carried to the sick house and died that night. I saw her coffin in the morning."

Long resumed questioning for the defense.

"How did you know that she died that night?"

"Mr. Hodge told me."

"Was she in irons?"

"She was taken out of chains that morning, to go into the kitchen."

Lisle asked, "Was it only for this day she was taken out of chains, or at other times?"

"I have seen her in chains in the field, and at night in the sick house, by way of confinement."

Then a member of the jury brought the questioning back to the subject of Prosper, inquiring, "Was Prosper supplied with food or not, after he was flogged?"

"I cannot say whether he was or not."

"Where was Prosper's house?"

"A little below the dwelling house."

Long resumed, asking, "You saw creepers on Prosper's body?"

"Yes."

"Did Mr. Hodge never give his negroes anything when they were confined?"

"I never knew him to do it while in a passion or even after. I never saw it done."

No one else had any questions and the first witness for the prosecution was finally excused.

Stephen McKeough was the next witness called for the Crown. McKeough, who had not referred to the death of Prosper in his deposition, was first questioned on *voire dire* by Tyson.

"Were you not at St. Croix?"

"I was."

"Were you not applied to, to come over and give evidence on this trial?"

"Some persons came to me, but did not apply to me to come over to give evidence."

"Did you leave your employment without knowing what it was you came for?"

"I did."

"Were you promised any other place?"

"I was not. I had permission from my employer to come over."

Then Horsford opened the examination for the Crown by asking, "Do you know the prisoner at the bar?"

"I do."

"Have you lived in his employ?"

"I have."

"Do you know all his slaves, and particularly Prosper?"

"I know Prosper."

"Was Prosper ever cartwhipped?"

"He was several times, and very severely, and at close quarters. He had one whipping so severe that I could put my finger in his side."

"Did you see him laid down?"

"I did."

"Did you see what you term close quarters?"

"I did not see the close quarters, but I saw the marks of them."

"Was he put in confinement after being flogged?"

"He was."

"Was he worked after this?"

"I saw him turned out to work. He was then capable."

"How long have you lived in the prisoner's employ?"

"I lived with him three times: this was the first time."

"How came you to know that Prosper was dead?"

"Mr. Hodge told me. I saw Prosper some days before he died, in a cruel state, so bad, I could not go near him for the blue flies."

"Were you living with the prisoner then?"

"No, but I used to go now and then, when Mr. Hodge sent for me. I saw Prosper then at the Gut; about two or three weeks before his death. I saw Mr. Hodge knock him down with a rock stone."

"Where was Prosper then?"

"He was doing something about the works."

"What was the cause of the prisoner's knocking him down?"

"It was about a bull."

"In what situation was Prosper then?"

"He was underneath Mr. Hodge, who took up a stone and knocked him down. When I saw him the last time I did not think he could live long."

"Why did you not think he could live long?"

"I thought so from hunger, watching in the cold, and confinement."

"Did the prisoner always treat Prosper with severity?"

"He was not always cruel to this man. He told me one time that Prosper was a very good negro, and if he had not him, he should not know what to do to cart his sugars. I thought he was a very good negro, and I observed that he deserved the character he gave him."

"By whose orders was the flogging inflicted?"

"I do not suppose it could be, but by Mr. Hodge's orders. If it had, Mr. Hodge would have inquired into it."

"What kind of a negro was Prosper?"

"A good looking strong negro."

"What was the cause of Prosper's death?"

"I believe the laceration to have been the cause."

Long rose to object that a witness on direct examination could not swear to his belief, only to facts of his knowledge.

The Solicitor General proceeded, "Have you had any conversations with Mr. John Skelton, Jr., relating to the prisoner?"

"I did mention to him Mr. Hodge's treatment of his slaves, years ago, when I left his employ the first time, and when I went to Paraqueto Bay. I begged him not to mention it again."

"Why did you enjoin secrecy?"

"Because I knew that if Mr. Hodge knew it he would not hesitate to take my life."

"Why did you think so?"

"I thought so by the manner he treated his slaves."

"Did anything more pass with Mr. Skelton?"

"I told him to beware of Mr. Hodge."

"Did Mr. Hodge say anything to you concerning Mr. Skelton?"

"He told me if I kept company with him, he would discharge me, as he was an unsafe man. I told Mr. Skelton of it the same day, at dinner, at my house, on Mr. Hodge's estate."

Horsford then opened another subject, asking, "Had Mr. Hodge a good gang of negroes when you first went to live with him?"

"He had a fine gang."

"How many negroes had he then?"

At this both Tyson and Long were up, objecting. Horsford withdrew the question. Tyson then began his cross–examination.

"Did you not go to St. Thomas?"

"I did, in 1809, from this place, in November."

"What was the cause of Mr. Hodge's discharging you?"

McKeough responded, "Because I was not severe enough. I told him that he prevented me, by being so severe himself, and if he allowed the overseer, driver and himself to punish he would not have a negro left."

"What did the prisoner say?"

"He said that if the work was not done to his will, he was satisfied so he heard the whip crack; his great pleasure was in cruelty."

Tyson then tried to impugn McKeough's character, in order to discredit his testimony. "How long," he asked, "did you live with Mr. Hodge the first time?"

"Six months, in 1805."

"Were not the keys, at times, in danger, in consequence of your being drunk? Did you not loose your hat and shoes?"

"I do not know or recollect that to be the case."

"Did not Mr. Hodge take the keys from you when you were in that state?"

"I do not know, nor recollect it."

"Where were you born?" Tyson asked in an offensive manner.

"Perhaps," McKeough replied angrily, "if I tell you, you would not know: in Ireland."

"How did you come over?"

"In a boat."

Tyson indicated his displeasure with the answer and pressed on, "In what situation did you leave Ireland?"

McKeough doubted whether he was bound to answer the question but replied, "I paid for my passage and left Ireland to recover property in St. Thomas, where I went about eleven years ago."

"Were you with Mr. Hodge in 1808?"

"I was, but not living with him; I was at the house and at the works frequently."

"Did you frequently see any strangers there?"

"The only person I saw there frequently was Mrs. Rawbone."

"Where were you when Mrs. Hodge died?"

"At the works."

"Was Mrs. Rawbone there?"

"She was."

"How far is it from the house to the works?"

"It is ten minutes walk, down hill."

"Did Perreen Georges live at Mr. Hodge's while you was there?"

"She did."

"Was she there at the time you were?"

"She was."

"What time was this?"

"It was in 1805. I went back in 1806. I then quitted him, and came again in 1807."

"In what situation was Perreen there, when Mrs. Hodge died?"

"As a kind of manager."

"How do you mean?"

"She attended and took care of the boiling house, which I call being a manager."

"Was Mrs. Hodge in the habit of going to the boiling house?"

"She was, frequently."

"For what purpose?"

"I do not know."

"Have you ever eaten at the same table with Mr. and Mrs. Hodge?"

"I have breakfasted, dined and supped with them."

"Do you mean at the great house, as his bottle companion?"

"I do. I have sat at table with them and Mrs. Rawbone."

"Have you," Tyson asked, "anything to say against Mr. Hodge in regard to his treatment of yourself?"

"Nothing," McKeough replied.

"Did not he ill treat you at any time?"

"He threatened to cartwhip me the last time I was with him. I asked him for payment several times."

"Did he ever threaten to kill you?"

"Never. I was armed with a good stick in case of need, but he did not offer me any violence."

"Have you ever had any quarrel with Mr. Hodge?"

"I have had a few words with him about pay. He has not paid me yet, but I don't intend to give up the debt, though I owe him no ill will in consequence of his not paying me. He owes me fifty–six pounds."

Lisle then examined on re–direct for the Crown.

"Do you feel any prejudice against Mr. Hodge for not paying you, or for anything else?"

"I do not."

"When you said you came in a boat, did you mean a sea boat, a ship?"

"I did mean so."

"Did Mr. Hodge tell you how Prosper died?"

"He did not."

"Did you assist in digging Mrs. Hodge's grave with Mr. Daniel Ross?"

"I did," McKeough replied, "because there were no proper negroes to do it."

With that his testimony was at an end. John Skelton, Jr. was then called to corroborate McKeough's conversations with him. Then Mark Dyer French was called to the stand. Counsel for the prosecution asked him, "Did you ride up to the prisoner's estate to enquire for the grave of Prosper, as one of the committee for carrying on this prosecution?"

"I did so in company with some others."

"Who pointed it out to you?"

"Perreen Georges."

"Was the grave opened?"

"It was."

"In what situation did you find the corpse?"

"The head was lower than any other of the bones, the legs crossed; but you had better refer to doctors who were there."

"What kind of grave was it?"

"It did not appear to be well dug. Some of the bones were near the surface."

"Where was the grave?"

"At the back door of Prosper's house."

"You say the head was lower and the grave seemed deeper about the head?"

"I do."

Tyson then cross-examined French, asking, "Was any notice given to Mr. Hodge to send an agent to attend?"

French replied, "No. Not to my knowledge."

"Did you see any irons or puddings?"

"No."

"Did Perreen say when she saw the corpse, the irons or crooks were on?"

"I understood so; and that this related to Prosper, I will not be positive."

Henry Lisle made a few observations summing up and the case for the Crown was closed.

Defense[17]

George Tyson, the Speaker of the Assembly of St. Christophers, made the opening statement for the defense.

"May it please Your Honors, gentlemen of the jury," he began, "I rise on the part of the gentleman at the bar, and I think before I sit down, I shall produce the most unexceptionable witnesses, to satisfy your minds as to the innocence of the prisoner."

He, like the prosecution, discussed the law of murder, and then he turned to discuss the witnesses presented by the Crown.

"It has been stated," he remarked, "by the learned counsel just set down, that he attributed the corroboration of evidence as an act of God! I say it was the act of man. These witnesses have been kept together for a length of time, and it will be admitted that when two people are put together for a length of time, they will with facility trump up a story and not only agree in it on being examined, but it may appear plausible.

"What has Mr. McKeough's conduct been? He treated the matter on his examination as a subject of mirth! He did not feel for three helpless children whom he would deprive of their only protection, their father!"

"McKeough is a guilty man—he is guilty of misprision of felony. This offense was said to be committed years ago. If this murder was committed, McKeough should have brought Mr. Hodge to justice. Mr. Hodge is brought forward at this remote period of time under the most cruel disadvantages. Witnesses who could come forward in exculpation are now no more; others he is deprived of by a variety of reasons.

"Can you believe McKeough when he tells you Mr. Hodge cared not for the work done by his negroes, provided the cart whip, the detestable lash of the cart whip, was heard by him! Is there any one in this court who can give credit to this declaration, that Mr. Hodge would sacrifice affluence, comfort, happiness, for the gratification of hearing the detestable cart whip? It is impossible that this be true, and yet he swears to it!

"McKeough has denied his having the keys on the occasion mentioned, or did not know he had them—this alone would impeach him. I shall be obliged to refer to many occurrences when I open the case on the part of Mr. Hodge. McKeough wishes to make it appear that he was intimate with—a bottle companion of Mr. Hodge! What will you say when I prove to you that he was never suffered to come into any other than a particular part of his house!

"I shall have occasion to bring Perreen's character into proper view. She tells you with regard to Margaret that she was so ill she was unable to cook the dinner and that she did it for her. Now suppose I prove that Margaret dressed the dinner that day—that she was talking to her of her character: that she ought to behave better and she would be a valuable negro; that on that day, when Perreen says she had the wound, she was well, and that at one o'clock in the morning Mr. Hodge was called up, attended to her kindly, but owing to some affliction of her breast, she died that day. Does this look like a wish for concealment on the part of Mr. Hodge, when it was notorious to all?

"If you find Perreen tripping, nay, falling in a matter foreign to the cause before us, must you not expect the same in what relates to it immediately? This humane creature could not bear to see the punishment of Prosper; she kept her post at the window until the flogging was ended, and then her stomach turned because there was not more flogging! Had she been humane as she would wish to be conceived, would she not have quitted her favorite window after the first lash of the whip?

"Much has been said about Prosper's death. Suppose I prove, and I can do it, that this negro was runaway at the time of this severe flagellation, and that Mrs. Rawbone, who was in the house, did not hear the lashes, though it is said it was done under the window. This man is certainly dead, he had secreted himself in his house, and when found was in such a putrid state, it was necessary to put him under ground on the nearest spot.

"I am instructed to say, the bones said to be Prosper's are now in court, and that some gentlemen went for the purpose of having them taken up! This is a horrible scene! let the pleasure of such an act be stated—I shall be satisfied if the propriety is made out—it is a crime and punishable.

"You have been told a story about a mango. Is it possible Mr. Hodge would sacrifice fifty joes for a mango fallen from a tree! Would he lacerate a negro for six shillings! Had Perreen been humane, she would have exerted herself to relieve him. Self-interest would have prevented it. Can you attribute it to resentment? Resentment against whom? His slave? A slave may excite anger, but surely not resentment. It is said that negroes were confined in the sick house for six or seven days without food; the same against those sick, as those by himself flogged? This sick house, you are told, was filled, and that they were all cut up! A monster could not have acted so.

"Mr. Hodge has resided in this country fifteen or twenty years; these charges may be said to be only the other day.

"Gentlemen who visited him, must see negroes in that state on an estate—you cannot therefore believe the witnesses. If he had no regard for himself, he would have some for a young family. These little innocents, his only comforts, he was deprived of in prison. Mr. Hodge was above escape—could he not have escaped? He was not apprehended—yes, he was, he went to the marshal for the purpose of being apprehended, and I hope he will receive the reward. Mr. Hodge has undergone unheard of hardships—loaded with irons. I never heard of a man, committing the grossest crimes, prevented seeing his friends, and thereby deprived of witnesses.

"Our case is plain—Prosper died a natural death, and was found in a house, not his own, in a putrid state. Gentlemen, what are you called upon to do? to sacrifice a fellow creature!—and on what evidence? McKeough and Perreen Georges!

"You feel he is not guilty because it is impossible such a character, as he is described to be, can be supposed to exist!

"This is not a question of mine or thine, of twenty shillings or twenty thousand pounds; it is not life—it is his honor, which is dearer, we are defending."

Counsel for the defendant began their defense of his honor—and his life—by calling as their first witness Penelope Hodge, the aged free black woman to whom the magistrates had first gone to obtain a statement.

Musgrave started gently, "Penny, relate what you know of Prosper."

"I don't know much about him, than that he is dead, which I heard."

"Do you know how he was buried?"

"He was dragged out of his house and buried."

"When did you see him?"

"I saw him a good while before his death. I can't say how long."

"Did you observe any marks of severity about him?"

"I did not, he was not cut up."

"Was he accustomed to run away?"

"He was."

"How long before his death did you see him?"

"I saw him a month before I heard he was dead."

"Did you see him frequently?"

"I did. He used to come to see me. I saw him before Mrs. Hodge died and after—heard he ran away."

"Was he sick?"

"He said he was."

"Did he complain of being beaten?"

"No."

"Had not Prosper been mad?"

"Yes."

The defense had no further questions of Penelope Hodge and Henry Lisle began the cross–examination for the prosecution, asking the old woman, "Do you know lawyer Lisle?"

"No."

"Did you ever see him?"

Penelope replied, "My sight is very bad. I have lost my left eye."

"How long has your sight been bad?" Lisle asked.

"Since Mrs. Hodge's death."

"Do you know how many days there are in a month, or how many months in a year?"

Penelope was silent. An observer thought that she was unable to answer the question.

"Do you know how many weeks there are in a month?"

"Four or five weeks."

"How many days are there in a week?"

"Six."

"Did any persons go up to you to take your deposition?"

"Yes, there were eight persons."

"Was," Lisle asked, "lawyer Lisle one of them?"

"My husband who was in the room told me so."

"Were you sworn? Did they make you take an oath?"

"No. I was not sworn."

Lisle then asked the defense counsel for Penelope's deposition, which she had given to Thomas Dougan on the fifth of March. After some argument the deposition was produced and read to the jury by Lisle.

Lisle then pointed out to the jury what he conceived to be contradictions between Penelope's deposition and her testimony in court, chiefly relating to her ability to recognize him. He closed by saying, "She has manifestly perjured herself, as you perceive, and nothing but her age and apparent imbecility protect her from punishment. You cannot pay the slightest regard to her evidence."

The members of the court were of the same opinion.

The defense then called Daniel Ross, who had been responsible for the Hodge estate while Arthur Hodge was living in England. Musgrave examined him.

"Did you know Prosper?"

"I did."

"What kind of negro was he?"

"He was," Ross answered, "an able and fine negro. I have understood that he is dead."

"Did you ever know him," Musgrave asked, "to be in a state of mental derangement?"

"I never did," Ross replied, raising doubts as to why the question had been asked.

"When did you see him last?"

"I saw him at the end of February or the beginning of March, 1808. I went in a boat where he was one."

"Do you know anything to the prejudice of McKeough?"

"I do not—he would take his soup; inclined to liquor."

"Do you know anything against Perreen?"

"Nothing."

"Have you seen McKeough in Mr. Hodge's house?"

"I have often."

"Was he on intimate terms with Mr. Hodge?"

"No."

"Have you ever seen him at his table?"

"I have once—on the day that Mrs. Hodge died, he dined and drank tea there."

"Do you recollect any other time?"

"I do not."

"Did Mr. Hodge place confidence in him?"

"Very little."

"Do you know whether Perreen had the care of the boiling house, acted as manager?"

"I don't recollect. I know she was there after McKeough quitted."

Musgrave's questions would have been of interest on a first meeting with the witness, but they had done nothing to acquit

Hodge of the charge of having murdered Prosper. He concluded, "Were the negroes disposed to runaway?"

Ross replied, "They were well disposed at that time, but when Mr. Hodge was in England they wanted privileges I would not grant, and I believe two–thirds absconded."

Horsford cross–examined for the Crown.

"Was Mr. Green then the manager?"

"He was."

"How many negroes," Horsford asked, "were there on the estate at that time?"

"There were 130 or 131—I saw the account of taxes today, which I paid."

"When was this?"

"In October of 1800; Mr. Hodge returned in 1803."

"Did the negroes, you mention to have runaway, return?"

"They did about a fortnight after and I cartwhipped the whole —with moderation."

"Did they conduct themselves well after that?"

"They did. I left it to their option to go away, or take punishment, and they chose the latter."

"Was Mrs. Rawbone with Mr. Hodge in 1808, after Mrs. Hodge's death?"

"She was. It was not her home, but she visited her friends."

"How did Mr. Hodge treat his negroes?"

Ross, though a witness for the defense, answered, "I cannot tell."

Thomas Llewellyn, a free mulatto carpenter, was the next witness called by the defense. On *voire dire* he was asked, "Have you had any later conversations with the prisoner?"

"I have."

"What was the subject of those conversations?"

"He begged me to recollect what I knew of him—and asked me as to particular days that I worked for him."

"Do you expect reward for appearing here?"

"No."

Musgrave then conducted the examination–in–chief.

"Did you do any work on the estate for Mr. Hodge?"

"I did, in 1805, 6 and 7."

"Did you see McKeough there in 1806?"

"I did."

"Did you see him there at any other time?"

"I did in 1807, but he was not living there then."

"Did you ever converse with McKeough and Perreen Georges?"

"Frequently."

"Did McKeough speak to you of Mr. Hodge?"

"He did. He would sometimes speak well of him, and at others call him severe; but said the negroes told him Mr. Hodge was severe."

"Was McKeough intimate with Mr. Hodge?"

"I thought he treated Mr. McKeough with such contempt that, were it me, I would not stay an hour with him."

"Did you ever see him at dinner with Mr. Hodge?"

"Never."

"Do you know anything of McKeough's character?"

"I do not."

"Did McKeough keep the keys?'

"He did not keep the key of the rum cellar; Mr. Hodge said he would not trust him with it."

"What was the situation there—was he likely to see acts of barbarity?"

"It was such that he could not go to the hill without being sent for; nor was he allowed to go into the yard without asking permission—nor I myself."

"Do you not know McKeough to be a drunkard?"

"I do not, except from what I have heard."

"Do you know anything against him?"

"Not from my own knowledge."

"During the time you were on the estate, did you observe any cruelty used towards the slaves?"

"I was there in 1805, 6 and 7 very constantly, but did not observe anything of cruelty to the negroes."

"Did you see Prosper?"

"I did, he was very weak. I asked him what was the matter—he said bad living."

"Do you know why McKeough and yourself were not allowed to go in the yard?"

"No."

Two other carpenters who had worked on the Hodge estate, Richard Moreton, a free black, and James Crook, a free mulatto, were also called to testify in an attempt to discredit McKeough and Perreen. So was Thomas Crook, a free mulatto shopkeeper who had been McKeough's landlord. He was asked of McKeough, "Have you ever observed him frequently to get drunk?"

"I have, sometimes at eleven o'clock in the forenoon."

"Do you know anything to discredit his testimony.?"

"I do not."

"Did you ever detect him in falsehoods?"

"No."

"Do you know Perreen?"

"I know nothing of her, or against her."

Mrs. Ann Arrindell was then called in an attempt by the defense to contradict Perreen's testimony concerning Margaret and thus throw her testimony concerning Prosper's death into question. She was asked, "Were you, at any time, a visitor at Mr. Hodge's?"

"I was."

"Did you know of Margaret's having cooked a dinner one day?"

"She did—remarkably well."

"Was she accustomed to have a pain in her stomach?"

"She was."

"Do you know anything respecting her death?"

"Mr. Hodge was knocked up by the servants, on that night, after we had all gone to bed. She died in the morning."

"Did you observe any marks of violence upon her?"

"None."

"What was Mr. Hodge's disposition towards his servants?"

"I never saw him irritated with them; he was a kind master, husband and father."

Lisle cross–examined for the Crown. "Do you recollect whether Margaret's handkerchief was on or off?"

"I do not."

"Was her mouth scalded?"

"I do not know."

"How do you know that Margaret cooked the dinner?"

"I supposed so, because she came for orders."

"How often have you visited Mr. Hodge?"

"I have been only four times."

"How long have you stayed on those occasions?"

"Four or five days at a time."

"Did you see Mr. McKeough or Perreen there?"

"I did not."

"Had Mr. Hodge any manager at that time?"

"I do not think he had any."

"Was Mr. Hodge attentive to his negroes when they were sick?"

"He was. He has often mixed medicines for them; he was clever that way."

"Do you know the cause of Margaret's death?"

"I can't be positive of what Margaret died; Mr. Hodge told me in the morning at the breakfast table that Margaret was dying or dead, I can't say which."

Horsford took over from his co-counsel, asking, "Did Mr. Hodge say she has a cramp or pain in her stomach?"

"He told me she was very ill. I think he said it was a cramp or pain in her stomach."

Defense counsel resumed, "What is your opinion of Mr. Hodge?"

"I can't say anything," Mrs. Arrindell replied, "but what is pleasant of Mr. Hodge, in justice to him, according to my conscience."

Lisle was up: "I shall go into evidence to prove the contrary."

Hodge's counsel objected to Lisle's remark, causing Horsford to argue that since the defense had called Mrs. Arrindell to support the defendant's character the prosecution had the right to present evidence concerning it. The court ruled that each party could examine as to general character.

Mr. Justice William Rogers Isaacs questioned the witness from the bench.

"Was any doctor called in to Margaret?"

"I don't know if there was any; there might be."

"Was it customary for Margaret to wear an handkerchief round her head?"

"I don't know; I think she did in general, but cannot say."

Mrs. Arrindell stepped down and Ann Rawbone, Hodge's sister, was called to the stand.

On *voire dire* Lisle objected to the testimony of Mrs. Rawbone, declaring "I can prove that she has declared she knew something that would hang her brother, but if she was brought forward to give evidence she would not say anything to injure him."

The court permitted her to testify and William Musgrave examined her, bringing the case back to Prosper momentarily, asking, "Did you know Prosper?"

"I did. He was runaway with a large pudding round his leg."

"Do you know of his death?"

"He was afterwards found in Scinda's house, dead, in a state of corruption, and buried near it."

"Did you see Perreen there?"

"I never saw her there."

"Do you know of Margaret's having cooked a dinner for Mr. Hodge?"

"I do. She cooked it very well."

"Do you know anything of her death?"

"I heard a noise at night, and my brother going out and coming in, and in the morning I heard from him that she died of a pain in her stomach."

"Was this not a family complaint?"

"It was. Her mother and sister died of it. Her mother nursed me and I have always been afraid of that pain."

"Do you know whether the puddings were taken off of Prosper?"

"I never heard of their being taken off."

"How long were you on the estate before he died?"

"Two or three months."

"Do you know of his being flogged?"

"I never knew of his being flogged."

"Was McKeough on the estate at that time?"

"He was not."

Lisle cross–examined, probing the relationship between the brother and sister.

"Did Mr. Hodge lock you up when he was about to punish negroes?"

"No."

"Did you say to someone that you could tell something to hang your brother, but if you were called on his trial you would say nothing to condemn him?"

"I sent a message by Dr. John West to my brother," Ann Rawbone replied, "to say that if he did not do something respecting my negroes, I would show a letter."

"What was the cause of the punishment of putting Prosper in irons?"

"Being a runaway. As he ran away with them, I suppose he had them on when he died."

Doctor William West was called and examined by Musgrave.

"Have you attended Mr. Hodge's estate?"

"I have the last six years, occasionally."

"Have you visited his sick house?"

"I have."

"Did you ever encounter any offensive smell there?"

"Not more than in others," he replied, contradicting Perreen. "It was as comfortable as they generally are. I have performed operations in it."

"Did you ever observe mutilated negroes there?"

"No."

After Dr. West had produced records of payments for having attended the Hodge estate, Horsford asked him, "Did you attend the estate by the year?"

"No—only when sent for."

"Were you called in to attend Prosper?"

"No."

Horsford then called Mrs. Rawbone to the stand.

"What do you know of McKeough?"

"I think him a drunkard and a liar."

"What induces you to think so?"

"I have heard it generally."

"From whom?"

"From Mrs. Ross and Mrs. Hodge."

More than a decade later the author of a description of the Virgin Islands would write, "I have heard . . . that family discord, in which McKeough and Hodge's own sister acted a prominent part, had its influence in McKeough's strong evidence of the prisoner's general cruelty towards his people." "A drunkard and a liar" she thought him.

Dr. John West was also called by the faltering defense.

"Did you know Prosper?"

"I know nothing of him. I never heard his name before this business."

As midnight approached the order and purpose of calling witnesses became more confused. Daniel Ross was recalled to the stand to be asked by Solicitor General Horsford in relation to Ann Rawbone's testimony, "Have you ever heard Mrs. Ross say anything of Mr. McKeough?"

He responded, "I declare I never did, nor do I believe she knows him, much less that she could have spoken ill of him to Mrs. Rawbone."

Ann Rawbone was recalled and asked, "What acquaintance had Mrs. Ross with Mr. McKeough?"

"I don't know how she knew him."

Juliana Roach, a free mulatto woman, took the stand and testified that Stephen McKeough and Perreen Georges both lived in Thomas Crooks' yard in July or August 1808, about the time of Prosper's death.

Jane Goodwin, another free mulatto woman, was called by the

defense and asked about Perreen, "Do you know anything of the character of Perreen Georges?"

"I know that she stole some clothes from her mistress when she was a slave."

"Do you know it of your own knowledge?"

"I do not know it of myself."

"Do you know anything against her since she has been free?"

"Nothing."

The last witness called by the defense was George Davis Dix, a Roadtown merchant and a member of the Council, who was examined on the bench.

"Was Mr. McKeough in your employ?"

"I employed him as a manager at Ballast Bay."

"Can you speak to his character?"

"He was an active, industrious man. I have no doubt of his veracity. I discharged him for intemperance in the evening—in 1804."

With that the defense rested.

Rebuttal[18]

It was now time for the Crown to present its rebuttal to the testimony of the witnesses called for the defense. Their efforts were to be concentrated on an effort to discredit Ann Rawbone's testimony in support of her brother.

The first witness called was Miss Jane Todman. Lisle conducted the examination.

"Have you heard Mrs. Rawbone make any declaration respecting the prisoner?"

"I heard Mrs. Rawbone say that her brother dare not disturb her, for she could hang him."

"When did this happen?"

"Just before she married Mr. Rawbone."

"Was she at variance with her brother?"

"She was, and until his imprisonment."

"Did she make any other declaration?"

"She said she would take a false oath to save her brother—she had seen nothing done, but could nevertheless hang her brother."

"Did Mrs. Rawbone tell you that when her brother was going to punish negroes he used to lock her up, and Mrs. Hodge?"

"No—but she said that on those occasions she would go into her room of herself."

Then the Crown called Mrs. Frances Pasea Robertson, the mother of William Cox Robertson, Musgrave's enemy who had written the letter which had formally opened the Hodge prosecution.

She was asked, "Did you hear Mrs. Rawbone make any declaration respecting her brother?"

"I did," she replied. "Mrs. Rawbone declared in my presence that she would perjure herself rather than condemn her brother."

"Did she say anything more?"

"At another time she said she could hang her brother. I gave her refuge in my house before her marriage. I mentioned that I was afraid of her brother and I observed to her that, being without a male protector (my son being in England and Mr. Smith at Ballast Bay), 'your brother may come with a side saddle and take you away.' Mrs. Rawbone answered, 'Don't fear, 'tis more than he dare do—I could hang him!' and she repeated that expression three times, holding up her finger."

"Have you conversed with Mrs. Rawbone on those subjects since 1808, and have you expressed yourself against Mr. Hodge with any animosity, or said you wished to see him hanged?"

"As I heard he spoke of me in a cruel manner, my feelings were wounded, and I did appeal on my knees to the Almighty to hear the prayer of the widow and orphan and let him have his deserts, if it was even with hemp. He has injured me, but if I have the opportunity, I will return good for evil—I am now here without animosity, and would go a thousand miles to serve him—for his children's sake."

Samuel Long cross–examined.

"Have you heard Mrs. Rawbone declare to you that she intended saying in court, what she mentioned to you?"

"I have understood so from her."

"Has not Mrs. Rawbone told you that what she knew was from negro information?"

"She has," Mrs. Robertson replied, thus throwing doubt on the admissibility of Ann Rawbone's testimony.

Lisle then asked, "Did she not tell you that she kept herself in her chamber to avoid being witness to these barbarities?"

"She did."

"At the time she said she could hang her brother did she mention negro testimony?"

"No."

Jane Todman was called back to the stand and repeated her previous testimony. Then John Rawbone, Hodge's brother–in–law, was called by the defense. Tyson asked him, "When was it that Mrs. Robertson made the declaration 'that she hoped Mr. Hodge would have his deserts, even if it were in hemp?'"

Rawbone, referring to March 5, replied, "It was on a Tuesday. Mrs. Rawbone was at Mrs. Robertson's, when the latter told Mrs. Rawbone that a warrant was issued out against her brother. Mrs. Rawbone was distracted. It was at that time Mrs. Robertson made the declaration you mention."

"Did you ever declare to anyone that Mrs. Rawbone was locked up by her brother?"

"Never. I said she went to her chamber."

"Did not you say to Mrs. Rawbone that she would make it worse for her brother?"

"I did not."

Horsford then called Jane Todman to the stand for a third time to ask her, "Was the declaration by Mrs. Rawbone made before or after the warrant was issued?"

"Before," she replied, and stepped down again.

John Stanley, a planter, was then called. Horsford asked, "Did Mr. Rawbone tell you that the prisoner made Mrs. Rawbone go down to her chamber when anything was going forward?"

"He did," Stanley answered.

"Did Mrs. Rawbone make any observations to you on meeting a negro with burnt lips on the road?"

"She did. She said, 'that is my brother's mark.'"

Prosper, for whose murder Hodge was on trial, seemingly having long since been forgotten by both sides, Horsford then asked Stanley, "Did she say anything to you respecting Jupiter?"

"She said that Jupiter had stolen some ratafia liqueur and was punished by burning in the mouth—that she heard his screams, and that he ran in her presence with his mouth in that state."

It was now after midnight on Tuesday morning, more than fourteen hours after the trial had begun. "The jury refreshed by mutual consent."

Perreen Georges was then recalled to the stand by Solicitor General Horsford. "Did Margaret," he asked, in response to Ann Rawbone's testimony, "complain of a pain in her stomach?"

"She did."

"Do you know the cause?"

"It proceeded from boiling water poured down her throat."

"How do you know this?"

"I saw the kettle of water."

"Who called for it?"

"Mr. Hodge—I heard the screeches, and saw her coming with her mouth burnt."

"How long was it before she died?"

"It was about two or three months. She spit blood a long time."

Tyson asked her, "What was Margaret doing in the kitchen?"

"Pounding minced meat."

"Was Joan there also?"

"She was."

"What happened after?"

"I helped Margaret; just as dinner went in she fell down and was carried into the sick house."

A member of the court asked, "Was Joan a good cook?"

"She was not."

"Were you doing what Margaret had to do?"

"I was."

McKeough was called back to the stand to be asked by Lisle, "Was Margaret a woman with a scalded mouth?"

"She was," he replied.

Robert Green, Hodge's former manager, with whom Perreen Georges and Stephen McKeough had been living since early March was called by the Crown.

"When you lived on Mr. Hodge's estate," he was asked, "how many negroes had he?"

"One hundred and thirty or one hundred and forty."

"When did you quit him?"

"In 1803, after he returned from England."

The prosecution called McKeough back to the stand for a third time. Henry Lisle closed the evidence by questioning him about the Hodge estate.

"Did Mr. Hodge ever tell you to mark down negroes as runaway whom he knew were dead?"

"He did."

"Did you keep a list of negroes?"

"I did. I gave him a list-board every morning."

"Was there a plantation book kept?"

"There was at one time. I kept one, but on Mr. Hodge finding things in it he did not wish, he destroyed it, and would not suffer any to be kept any longer."

"Did he ever sell any negroes?"

"Not more than one or two."

"Did he ever sell any to Mr. Forbes?"

"I don't recollect."

"Do you know of any runaways at Santo Domingo?"

"There are two or three at Santo Domingo. I recollect Thomas being runaway."

"Have you frequently seen negroes on the estate with puddings and crooks?"

"I have."

"Have you ever seen any with two puddings on each leg, and a crook?"

"One negro, I believe, named Fortune, Mr. Hodge said he could not bring him down."

"Was his mouth burnt?"

"It was."

"Do you believe Mr. Hodge to be a cruel man?"

"I cannot say otherwise than that he was cruel, from his treatment of his negroes."

Argument[19]

It was now time for counsel to make their closing arguments to the jury. George Tyson spoke for the defense. He began by referring to the lateness of the hour and the exhausted state in which he found himself. He then reviewed the testimony of McKeough and Perreen Georges "and commented upon it at length," according to the reporter.

Then he turned to the testimony of the witnesses for the defense. "He could not give up the testimony of Mrs. Rawbone," the reporter wrote, "on account of her relationship to Mr. Hodge. A father may give testimony against a son, a brother against his sister, it could not be affected. He admitted regard on the part of relations generally, but *they* had had family quarrels. She had charged Mr. Hodge with being the cause of her losing four negroes.

"Before her reconciliation with him, she had declared that her intention or meaning referred to those negroes; Mrs. Rawbone was contrasted with Mrs. Robertson; the proceeding of the latter lady had been violent in the extreme. She entertained impressions against Mr. Hodge, and they had operated on her mind to that degree, that she threw herself on her knees in an agony, and recommended him to his deserts—hemp! qualified after by saying 'if he deserved it.' She had fervently prayed for the destruction of Mr. Hodge; said afterwards she was not prejudiced against him, and would do anything to serve him. She certainly was prejudiced; Mr. Rawbone gave a different account.

"The declaration of Mrs. Rawbone was made in an agony of

grief; she had been in that state two or three hours—it was then and only then, and under the excruciating feelings she was over-powered by, she said '*if* I knew anything of my brother, I would perjure myself rather than injure him.'

"Mr. Tyson then recapitulated and contrasted the whole of the evidence, and commented upon it at great length."

Solicitor General Paul Horsford made the closing address to the court and jury on the part of the Crown.

"May it please your Honors, gentlemen of the jury," he began, "it is now past two o'clock on Tuesday morning, and the trial of the prisoner at the bar, for the murder of his slave Prosper, com-menced yesterday morning at the hour of ten. Sixteen hours have been consumed in the investigation of this most horrid, this most barbarous act of wanton cruelty—cruelty which has led to death.

"Gentlemen, you may easily conceive that after the watchful attention necessary to be given to a cause of this importance, through all its shifts and changes, that nature must be almost exhausted; but, I trust, by the assistance of the Almighty, whose laws I am now advocating, that the zeal which I feel will enable the energies of my mind to support the feebleness of my body.

"With the aid of my God, I shall be able to paint the murderer at the bar, as he really is, shocking to behold: By the command of the representative of Majesty, I present myself before you, as the advocate of humanity, to support the wholesome and beneficial laws of civil society."

Horsford then reviewed the evidence with great style and at a length which belied his claimed exhaustion, contrasting "this rich, but hard hearted man . . . this favorite of fortune, child of afflu-ence" with "his poor distressed negro, whose labors had contrib-uted to his luxuries."

He searched for a motive for Hodge's actions and found that "The depravity of his heart has made him even regardless of self–interest. His ferocious and black heart has caused him to murder his defenseless slave, and to the destruction of his own property."

He referred to the testimony of Perreen Georges and Stephen McKeough, declaring, "If you believe these witnesses there is an end to the defense set up by the prisoner's counsel; it rests altogether on the credibility of their testimony, which stands firm and unshaken."

"Another, but indirect defense," he continued, "is that persons, enemies to Mr. Hodge, have conspired together to do him an injury, that through their exertions this prosecution has been instituted.

"The first charge that is brought against the prisoner by affidavit is by Mr. Cox Robertson, who was at one time the friend and companion of Mr. Hodge. Whether these former friends have quarreled or not, or whether the accuser of Mr. Hodge, discovering the malignity of his heart and the atrocity of his acts and deeds, or whether the accusation proceeded in the first instance from a motive of ill–will or revenge, is not an object of minute inquiry on your part—provided the fact charged in the indictment be true, and proved to your satisfaction, either by positive testimony, or circumstantial evidence, or the one supported by the other.

"Gentlemen, you must recollect how closely the counsel on the part of the Crown confined themselves, in the examination of witnesses, to the specific, to the individual charge or murder laid in the indictment. But notwithstanding this proper and extreme caution on their part, in performing a duty between the King and his subject, what came out upon the cross–examination of our witnesses by the prisoner's counsel? In an attempt to invalidate the testimony, given on the part of the prosecution, they prove by their own showing that he is also guilty of the murder of an unfortunate female slave of the name of Margaret by pouring into her mouth, and down her throat, boiling water out of a tea kettle and by other barbarous and diabolical inflictions of cruelty.

"It is true, gentlemen, an indictment is now ready, and on the table, to be presented to the grand jury for the murder of Margaret, as well as seven other indictments for murder, all of which, gentlemen, no doubt you have been informed of by general report. We should not have brought them forward in aid of the present indictment, now at issue, nor have mentioned them, had we not been authorized to do so in consequence of their being touched upon by the prisoner's counsel, and mentioned with the hope and expectation of entrapping our witnesses. My learned friends judiciously refrained from going any further than the case of Margaret, finding as they advanced they stepped into blood, shed by the murderer at the bar!

"Gentlemen, you have attentively followed me in this melancholy labyrinth—this vale of horrors! I feel grateful, and, in mercy, I wish I could present you with a scene less dreadful and gloomy than this Golgotha."

Then he reviewed, in some detail, as Lisle had at the opening of the trial, the law of homicide and murder as the crime was defined by the common law of England and by the Leeward Islands Melioration Act. He went on, "Gentlemen, I have lived long enough in this western part of the globe, since I have arrived at the mature period of life, to enable me with experience to form a correct judgment on this subject; and I do most boldly affirm, that the slaves in these colonies, are at least as happy as the peasantry in England, when they possess humane masters. No instance like the present is within the knowledge of man. This case, for the honor of the world, has no parallel."

Horsford turned to a new topic.

"The advocate for the prisoner has attempted to address your feelings, knowing that according to your reason and judgment, guided by the evidence and the law, you must find the prisoner guilty. He tells you, you will by a verdict of guilty, deprive three innocent children of their only parent.

"Gentlemen, I must admonish you that you have no right to indulge your feelings at the expense of your conscience. You have taken a sacred oath to do impartial justice between the king and the prisoner."

Then he turned to the murder of Prosper, urging, "Dismiss for a time from your minds the evidence that has been produced on the part of the Crown—and out of his own mouth shall he be condemned! The defense set up to rebut the charge of murder contained in the indictment is that the deceased Prosper died by the visitation of God or that he was guilty of self–murder.

"It is admitted that he is dead. Then what occasioned that death? It is stated that he ran away from his master's service, that he was apprehended, that he was punished with the usual and proper instruments, that irons were put upon him, that he was placed in confinement, that he illegally broke his prison, effected his escape, concealed himself in his house, where he remained shut up to avoid discovery until he died.

"You will recollect that Prosper's character stood high in the estimation of his master. What then should make a good slave a runway? The answer is, hard usage. He is apprehended and punished. What should induce any reasonable creature who had already suffered the corporal punishment which his crime merited to break his prison and commit a new offense? The natural answer is, the fear of further punishment, on continuation of imprisonment, which well known experience had taught him was never ending! According to Mrs. Rawbone's evidence, after his flogging he is confined in the pestilential prison with irons, called puddings, upon his legs. What must be the feelings and sufferings of that slave, who shall become a voluntary prisoner and die an agonizing death from want rather than face his inhuman master. Gentlemen, you will say, if this is the death Prosper died, which is proved by their own witnesses, the prisoner at the bar murdered him!

"Has not the testimony of Mrs. Rawbone, sister to the prisoner, been completely done away by the evidence of Mrs. Robertson? Mrs. Robertson has spoken feelingly, but she has spoken truth. . ... The finger of God has pointed out the son of this lady to be, with his divine aid, the avenger of her wrongs. He is his first accuser; he brings to view in a legal light that which was long known but remained unnoticed and uninvestigated for want of proof to bring conviction home to the murderer's door.

"Your injured country stands disgraced in the eyes of her sister colonies for criminal supineness. It is now struggling to wash away the imputed stain of disgrace—what men could do, has been done. You now represent that country and by your verdict you are to determine what regard you pay to the laws of God and the laws of the land.

"I am much inclined," Horsford continued, "to think from the manner in which the prisoner's counsel conducted themselves at the commencement of the prosecution that they believed him to be innocent, or that the legal evidence, on the part of the Crown, would have been insufficient to support the charge laid in the indictment. But I possess little knowledge of the human mind if their sentiments are not woefully altered and will confidently predict that if they filled your places they would think, as I am sure you do, that beyond any doubt, the prisoner is guilty.

"The general character of the prisoner at the bar is well known to you. His cruelty is notorious. Mr. Ross and Mr. Green inform you that eight years ago he was the owner of near one hundred and fifty negroes. How many, gentlemen, to your own knowledge, has he now upon his estate? That, coming within your private knowledge, is good proof. I am informed there are not more than thirty-five remaining. Has this deficiency been accounted for? Has there been an epidemic disorder in the Virgin Islands, which could have destroyed so great a number of the slaves? None has been proved. Has there been a like mortality among the slaves of any other proprietor within your knowledge? None has been proved. Has he proved runaways beyond two or three, or the sale of more than one? What says the medical gentleman, who occasionally attended the prisoner's slaves? Did he see Prosper, or did he see Margaret? or did he see any of the slaves, which the prisoner is charged with having murdered? No. The doctor never saw any of them. If these deaths would have borne the test of enquiry why was not the coroner applied to, to hold an inquest on their bodies? What was Mrs. Rawbone's conversation to her husband upon meeting a negro with his lips burnt off? That the unfortunate wretch was her brother's slave, for that was his mark!

"The dawn of the morning warns me of the time I have occupied. Let not the sun that is about to rise, set, and find you not at peace with your consciences. I know that the jury box is filled with men of religion. Let me remind you of the words of the Mosaical Law, as well as God's precept to Noah: 'whoso sheddeth man's blood, by man shall his blood be shed.'

Moreover, 'you shall take no satisfaction for the life of a murderer who is guilty of death, but he shall be put to death; for the land cannot be cleansed of the blood that is shed therein, but by the blood of him that shed it.'"

Richard Hetherington and Chief Justice Robertson charged the jury as the sun rose. Hetherington told them, "You have heard the evidence, adduced by persons, as I believe, entitled to full credence. You have heard the law, as laid down in the books, respecting murder. The law makes no distinction between master and servant. God created white and he created black creatures; and as God makes no distinction in administering justice, and to him each is alike, you will not, nor can you alter your verdict, if murder has been proved— whether on white persons or on black persons, the crime is equally the same with God and the law. If you believe that murder has been committed, as I do, you must find the prisoner guilty. If not, you must acquit him of the crime alleged against him. The fact and the evidence rest on you to determine on now—whether guilty or not guilty."

Robertson concluded his charge by referring to the witnesses, saying, "The prisoner's sister, however excusable her attachment to her brother might be, is reprehensible, as is the old black woman, Penelope Hodge, who made the deposition. The credit of the witnesses remains for you to decide on, and you will, when you retire, consider the subject as its importance merits and discharge your duty free from prejudice or favor, as you, by your oaths are bound to do, and bring in your verdict accordingly."

Then, at last, the defendant, Arthur Hodge, rose to address the jury.

"Gentlemen," he began, "as bad as I have been represented, or as bad as you may think me, I assure you that I feel support in my afflictions from entertaining a proper sense of religion. As all men are subject to wrong, I cannot but say that principle is likewise inherent in me.

"I acknowledge myself guilty in regard to many of my slaves, but I call to God to witness my innocence in respect of the murder of Prosper.

"I am sensible the country thirsts for my blood, and I am ready to sacrifice it."

Verdict

After Hodge had completed his statement—sometime after five in the morning—the jury retired to consider the case.[20] They returned at about eight o'clock with their verdict: "that the said Arthur Hodge is guilty of the felony and Murder aforesaid."[21] They also found, so that his estate would not be forfeited, "that he at the time of committing the said felony and Murder, or at any time since, had no goods or chattels, lands or tenements to the knowledge of the said Jurors."[22] Having told that lie, they went on, "And the majority of the said Jurors recommend the Prisoner to Mercy."[23]

Horsford moved that judgment be entered on the verdict. The court asked Hodge "if he had anything to say why Judgment of Death should not be passed upon him." His counsel then asked for a postponement of sentencing in order to permit them time to present the jury's recommendation for mercy to Governor Elliot. The court refused to grant any delay[24] and, as the reporter recalled, "Mr. Chief Justice Robertson, in the usual form, and in the most impressive and affecting manner, pronounced the awful sentence of the law on the prisoner, namely, to be hanged by the neck on Wednesday, the eighth of May following, until he was dead, on a spot near unto the common prison."[25]

13

Execution and Reflection:
"The Awful Signal"

Governor Hugh Elliot refused to consider the jury's recommendation of mercy for Arthur Hodge, explaining his motives in a letter to his wife,

> "By a majority of the jury he was recommended to mercy, and that mercy it was in my power to have granted by suspending the execution of his sentence till the King's pleasure should be known. But alas! there were no grounds which could justify me in acceding to the strange recommendation of the majority of the jury, neither would any of the judges second it. The unfortunate man would have been tried upon five other indictments, some of them still more atrocious than the one on which he was found guilty, and his general character for barbarity was so notorious that no room was left for me even to deliberate."[1]

Elliot imposed martial law upon the colony and put the militia on permanent duty—thus transforming William Gordon, Clerk of the Court, into Colonel William Gordon. He arranged with Captain Russell of *H.M.S. Cygnet* to supply the militia with arms and to have a party of marines and armed seamen ready to land if they should be needed to support his authority.[2]

On the day the trial ended Elliot accepted the resignation of

Thomas Thomasson as President of the Virgin Islands because of his old age and ill health. He was replaced by Richard Hetherington, the senior member of the Council, who, together with the Chief Justice, had presided at the trial.[3]

Hodge's proponents were busy following the trial. Elliot wrote to Margaret, "Judge of the distress I have been exposed to the whole of this last week by the petitions of the prisoner, and the personal applications of his relatives."[4]

He also reported to Lord Liverpool "that some of the prisoner's relations had tampered with the master of a vessel to carry him off in case they could have succeeded in releasing him from jail."[5]

Should the pleas for a stay of execution and the attempts to escape both fail "the prisoner," who had mixed medicines for his slaves and "was clever that way,"[6] "had secretly procured arsenic with a view of putting a period to his existence." Hodge was deterred from suicide "in consequence of the religious impressions made upon him by the Reverend Mr. Kerie," whom Elliot had brought from Antigua, "and under which impression he acknowledged he had been deterred from adding one sin more to the number of his former crimes."[7]

Abraham Mendes Belisario, who published the record of Hodge's trial, reported that,

> "During the time allowed the prisoner for regulating his worldly concerns and making his peace with his God he was constantly attended by the Reverend Mr. Kerie, of St. Christophers, and also Mr. Turner and Mr. Jewett, preachers attached to the Society of Methodists. He appeared sincere and fervent in his prayers during the short time allowed him in this world."[8]

Belisario and *The Times* of London both published accounts of the execution. "On the evening preceding his execution," *The Times* reported, "he took leave of his three young children, which so overpowered him as to make a matter of doubt whether he would ever be restored to tranquillity. In the morning, however, he was calm, and acquired still greater fortitude by receiving the sacrament. He walked with firmness to the place of execution," behind the jail.[9] He was accompanied, Belisario added, "by the Reverend Mr. Kerie and Mr. Jewett. . .. When he reached the fatal spot he addressed some individuals, whom he singled out in the crowd, and begged they would pardon any injuries they had received at his hands. After spending some time in devotion, he ascended the platform, where he again prayed, and his last words were addressed, generally, to all who surrounded him to forgive him and to join in prayer for his eternal salvation. He then gave the awful signal and was instantly launched into eternity."[10] "Thousands of persons," *The Times* concluded, "witnessed the awful spectacle, some of whom rather indecently expressed exultation."[11]

*   *   *

Elliot wrote Hodge's obituary in his letter of the next day to his wife Margaret:

> "Yesterday the fatal sentence of the law was carried into effect, and thus perished a man born to affluence, connected with families of distinction in England. He had been three times married; has left several children. He had been in the Army, had a liberal education and lived in what is called the Great World. His manners and address were those of a gentleman. Cruelty seems in him to have been the effect of violence of temper, and habit had made him regardless of the death or suffering of a *slave*. God grant that this severe example may teach others in the West Indies to dread a similar fate, should they forget that *slaves* are their *fellow creatures* and that their lives are protected by the Laws both of England and the Colonies."[12]

*   *   *

The execution took place at noon. At ten o'clock Governor Elliot had assembled the Council at the Courthouse to be prepared for any emergency. When word "was brought that the business was over," as Heydinger put it,[13] the militia were paraded and the Governor's thanks for their service was read by Colonel Gordon.

"The alarm gun was then discharged," Elliot wrote to Liverpool the next day, "as a signal that martial law had ceased and the militia returned to their respective homes."[14]

"The state of irritation," he continued, "and I may almost say, of anarchy, in which I have found this Colony, rendered the above measures indispensable for the preservation of tranquillity, and for insuring the due execution of the fatal sentence of the law against the late Arthur Hodge. Indeed, it is but too probable that, without my presence here as Commander in Chief, in a conjecture so replete with party animosity, unpleasant occurrences might have ensued."[15]

In the days following the execution Elliot busied himself reforming the government of the Virgin Islands, addressing the Council and Assembly and receiving their replies—including the ever–welcome provision for his salary—and contemplating the events of the past month.[16]

On May 17 he wrote to Lord Liverpool to arrange payment to Solicitor General Horsford for his services. In his dispatch he referred to "the universal attention which the trial of the late Arthur Hodge has attracted in the West Indies, and the deep impression which his fate will make upon the minds of the Planters and their servants." He suggested that, "When Your Lordship will have remarked that notwithstanding the enormity of the guilt of Arthur Hodge, so unusual an incident took place as a recommendation to mercy by a majority (which I now understand to have been seven) of the Jury, Your Lordship will be sensible of the peculiar difficulties by which the course of justice is liable to be obstructed in the West Indies in a cause where a Master is arraigned for the murder of his slaves by severe treatment." That such difficulties had been overcome in this case he attributed to the "profound judgment" of Mr. Horsford, which had resulted in "the greatest triumph which has yet been gained by law and justice over local prejudices and deep–rooted habits. . ... The lives of thousands of our fellow creatures, born to bondage," he concluded, "are now proved to be under the special protection of law, and are henceforth to be considered as sheltered from cruelty and oppression, by the verdict of a colonial jury."[17]

Elliot returned to the subject in another dispatch which he dictated for Liverpool the following day. "My Lord," he began, "it is with regret I am still to dwell upon so melancholy a subject as the trial of the late Arthur Hodge, and the circumstances with which it has been attended." Explaining his refusal to postpone the execution, he referred to "the situation of the Country, put under martial law," which "made it also impracticable for me, with a due regard for the preservation of tranquillity, to grant even a respite of a week. The militia being composed partly of Whites and partly of free coloured people, between whom the seeds of dissension have long been sown, and the Officers having only been appointed since my arrival in this island, I was imperiously called upon to put an end to the existence of martial law as speedily as possible in order that the Colony might resume its usual mode of administration before any untoward accident should have occurred that might have occasioned a misunderstanding between the White population and the free people of Colour."[18]

Probably referring to Richard Hetherington, Elliot went on, "One of the most respectable inhabitants of this community, who owns a neighbouring property, has assured me, that the habits of severity towards his servants, had attained such a height in the late Arthur Hodge that but a small proportion of his Negroes died a natural death. What then, My Lord, is to be thought of a state of society where such enormities were not likely to have ever been subjected to public investigation, had it not been for the accidental and personal quarrels of this guilty being with some of his former associates and friends!!!

"Would to God that I could consider a disposition to cruelty in the West Indies as having been confined solely to one individual, but much I fear that the skeleton of a Negro arrayed in chains would not be the only proof the uncovered graves would discover of victims to tyranny and oppression.—Mutilated limbs and broken hearts have withdrawn thousands of bondsmen from the miseries of a life of servitude.

"The day perhaps will come when a British Legislature may think it expedient to define with precision, and with Christian benevolence, the extent of the rights which one human being can exercise over his fellow creatures. In the meantime, I trust that the public example held up by the condign punishment of the late Arthur Hodge will, at least, serve as a check to many who conceived that death ensuing from severity of punishment inflicted by violence of temper upon a slave would not be considered in the eye of Law as heinous and atrocious murder."[19]

14

Impact on History:
"The Hand of God"

In July 1807, shortly after Parliament's passage of the bill abolishing the slave trade, the leaders of the campaign for its passage joined in establishing the African Institution. Its purpose was "to repair the ruin and degradation" which had been visited upon Africa by promoting trade with and education in and about that continent. The Institution's membership roster included men of great distinction. Its president and patron was William Frederick, Duke of Gloucestor, the King's nephew. The Archbishop of Canterbury and the Bishop of London were members, as were parliamentary leaders William Pitt, Henry Brougham and William Wilberforce. Leaders from the abolition fight included Thomas Clarkson, James Stephen and Zachary Macauley, who served as the Institution's secretary. One of its prime interests during its early years was oversight of the administration of the Abolition Act. It did not at first formally concern itself with West Indian slavery, which its leaders quietly hoped would now wither and eventually die.[1]

The Spanish colony of Trinidad had been taken by the British in 1797, and ceded by the Spaniards in 1802.[2] For a decade argument raged between the British planters who were settling there, desiring the establishment of a colonial government after the model of the older British colonies, with internal self–government, and those who favored the preservation of Spanish law or direct administration from London. The abolitionists in England opposed the establishment of internal self–government because they feared that the colonials would oppose abolition and amelioration.[3]

Late in 1810 Lord Liverpool, the Colonial Secretary, advised the Governor of Trinidad of the government's decision not to introduce a local legislature in the conquered colony.[4] It was Liverpool's intent to justify this decision by exposing to Parliament examples of maladministration in the older British Caribbean colonies. In this he was joined by James Stephen of the African Institution, who had determined that the next step in easing the circumstances of the slaves should be the establishment of a registry which would record their actual number and provide a means of monitoring their condition.[5]

Pursuing this objective, Stephen brought to Liverpool's attention the Huggins case in Nevis.[6] Liverpool caused Hugh Elliot's correspondence concerning that case to be published and presented to the House of Commons.[7] Later acknowledging that the publication of Elliot's dispatches on the state of colonial government was bound to cause him "resentment" and "personal inconvenience," Liverpool justified his decision by referring to "the able comments which they contained on the civil and judicial institutions of the islands under your Government, their immediate references to the subject then under discussion, the weight due to the testimony which they bear, not less from the character than from the situation of the person by whom it is given."[8] The Huggins papers were presented to the House of Commons on July 1, 1811, with large extracts having already been published in the London press on June 15.[9]

The news of Hodge's arrest, trial and execution fit neatly into Liverpool's plans. On June 26 Elliot's correspondence concerning Hodge was ordered to be printed by the House of Commons.[10] The House of Lords did likewise on July 1.[11] A report of the trial and execution appeared in *The Times* of London on July 9 and in *The Globe* on July 12. The story created a sensation.

Both the July 1811 issues of *The Christian Observer*,[12] edited by Zachary Macauley, secretary of the African Institution, and the influential *Gentleman's Magazine*[13] carried long reports of the trial with summaries of the depositions of Perreen Georges and Stephen McKeough. *The Christian Observer* reported that Mrs. Hodge had died insane. It also referred to the former close friendship between George Martin and Arthur Hodge and stated that Martin had once frustrated an attempt by a temporary resident of Tortola "to bring Hodge to justice for some gross acts of oppression towards a free person of colour."

The Christian Observer also printed in full Lord Liverpool's reply of June 20 to Governor Elliot's dispatches. Liverpool had conveyed to Elliot the Prince Regent's "high satisfaction" with his conduct and his agreement with Elliot's decision not to accept the jury's recommendation of mercy.[14] *The Christian Observer* closed its report by alluding to Trinidad and the fact that "in the West Indies . . . British laws mean neither more nor less than the communication of a power to the white inhabitants to oppress, at their pleasure, the slaves and free people of colour."

Abraham Belisario, a Roadtown merchant and long–time resident, had attended the trial as a member of the Grand Jury and made a transcript of the proceedings. This and copies of the depositions and other documents he had certified by President Richard Hetherington and sent, with the approval of the Virgin Islands Council and Assembly, to his brother J. M. Belisario in London to be published.[15] *The Trial of Arthur Hodge* was published in September. Two editions were printed in London and a third edition appeared in the United States the following year.

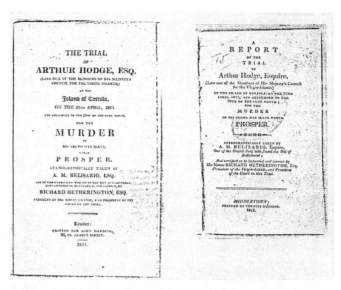

Title Pages of English and American Editions of *The Trial of Arthur Hodge*

The *Trial*, together with two pamphlets supporting the planter interest, was the subject of a lengthy article in the *Edinburgh Review* for November[3] . The *Review* was edited by Henry Brougham, M.P., who also was a member of the African Institution. One of the tracts reviewed with Belisario's *Trial* was written, according to its author, as an "antidote" to the unfavorable impression of West Indians that had resulted from the Hodge trial and the publication of the papers connected with it. Together with a second pamphlet, possibly by the same author, it painted a favorable impression of West Indian slavery, which was found to be superior to a life of freedom in Africa. The abolition of the slave trade was deplored. In an extraordinary statement the author remarked that "This very abolition, which preaches humanity, destroys, in the breast of the poor slaves, the cheering hope and expectation of ever meeting again their nearest ties."[17]

The *Review* recommended that those appointed to be West Indian governors, military commanders and judges should own no property in the colonies and not be allowed to acquire such property. Constant communication should be maintained with the government in London and all incidents of mistreatment should be fully and instantly investigated. Those who opposed such measures were reminded "that the enemies of reform are the true abettors of revolution."[18]

The *Annual Register* for 1811 included the Hodge trial as one of three West Indian events it thought worthy of mention in its review of the history of the year; the others being an insurrection in Martinique and the crowning of Henri Christophe as King of Haiti.[19]

The Hodge trial, including McKeough's testimony concerning the listing of dead slaves as runaway and the destruction of the plantation book,[20] provided a powerful argument for James Stephen's suggested registry.[21] On March 26, 1812, the government ordered the registration of all slaves in Trinidad.[22]

The African Institution, whose leadership had brought about Parliament's outlawing of the slave trade, determined on empire–wide registration as the next step in their campaign to improve the condition of the West Indian blacks and so prepare them for freedom. As before, it proceeded slowly and methodically.[23] In 1815 Stephen published his *Reasons For Establishing A Registry of Slaves In The Colonies.*[24] Wilberforce first introduced the necessary legislation in June of that year. Meanwhile, the government was urging the individual colonies to enact similar measures.[25] Brougham argued in the *Edinburgh Review* that annual registration would lead to early exposure of another Hodge affair.[26]

A pamphlet war was initiated, with the Institution sponsoring the publication of a series of eight *West–Indian Sketches.*[27] The planter interest replied with a series of *Antidotes To West Indian Sketches.*[28] Two of the *Sketches* and one of the *Antidotes* were devoted in their entirety to the Hodge case. Argument raged as to whether it was outraged Tortolan justice or party animosity that had brought Arthur Hodge to trial years after his crimes had been committed.

Universal, annual registration of slaves was approved by Parliament in 1819.[29] No slave could be purchased and no loan could be secured by a master's property right in his slave unless the slave was registered.

The memory of Arthur Hodge lived on on both sides of the Atlantic.[30] His name would be heard in the parliamentary debates of the 1820s which led to the final act of emancipation.[31] In a West Indian travel narrative of the 1830s reference was made to Tortola and the Bazaliel Hodge estates there with the footnote: "The name of Hodge is not to be mentioned in connection with this island, or indeed with the West Indies, without reminding one of him, who expiated with his life the crime of murder."[32]

A century later a visitor to Tortola would record the words of an aged black resident: "In slavery days the black man's life count for nothing; but after the time of Hodge a black man's life count the same as a white man."[33]

*   *   *

William Musgrave, once Senior King's Counsel in the Virgin Islands, left Tortola, at Elliot's direction, within a few days after the trial.[34] Elliot had told Liverpool that, "After mature investigation of the charges alleged against Mr. Musgrave, it is with pain I must acknowledge that they appear to me to have been but too well founded, and admit of no better excuse than indiscretion and the incentives of party–heat and animosity."[35]   But three years later he would support Musgrave's petition for an appointment as King's Counsel in Antigua, declaring that "it was indeed the office I meant to confer upon him after he had been called to the Bar in England, as an indemnification for his having quitted Tortola at my request, on account of the party animosity which prevailed in that island, and which in my opinion could not be allayed while Mr. Musgrave continued to practice there."[36]

Musgrave was to serve as Attorney General of Antigua and later became a judge at the Cape of Good Hope, where he died.[37]

George Martin died before the decade was out, leaving great wealth in land and slaves to the children of his slave mistresses.[38]

William Rogers Isaacs, who had served as one of the judges at the Hodge trial, lived on for many years, becoming—with his partner, William George Crabb—one of the principal attorneys and managers for the absentee landlords who controlled more and more of the islands as the British mortgage holders foreclosed on the planters' estates, President of the Virgin Islands (while Crabb was Chief Justice) and occupant of a large number of other offices.[39] Thirty years later, after emancipation, it would be said that "Mr. Isaacs and his lady are much beloved in this island. They are looked up to for much that is good and charitable."

Chief Justice James Robertson died in Tortola in 1818, at the age of sixty-seven.[40] In 1814 he had returned to Europe for his first visit in many years. Sixty of the "people of Colour residing in the Virgin Islands" presented him, on that occasion, with an address "begging leave to assure you we hold you in the highest esteem." They were joined by the white planters and merchants, who referred to Robertson's "long tried abilities, justice and impartiality as a judge, your kind and condescending manners as a gentleman, and your universal friendly disposition towards all ranks." The Royal Attorney General of Georgia during the American Revolution had traveled a long road.[41]

The Earl of Liverpool, the Colonial Secretary, became Prime Minister in 1812 following the assassination of Prime Minister Spencer Percival in the lobby of the House of Commons.[42]

Hugh Elliot received a private note from Lord Bathurst, the new Colonial Secretary, in the summer of 1813, telling him that he was being recalled from the Governorship of the Leeward Islands in order to be sent to Java, which his brother, Lord Minto, had taken from the Dutch. Both the government and the East India Company, Bathurst wrote, referring to public servants who gained fortunes in India, "hope to see you a Nabob at last."[43]

While back in England Elliot conferred with Bathurst on the future form of government for the Leeward Islands, thus fulfilling the promise of his first speech in Antigua. Bathurst was persuaded to split the Leeward Islands into two governments, headquartered in Antigua and St. Christophers. Elliot would have preferred establishing a separate government for Anguilla and the Virgin Islands, but realized that this was not fiscally sensible.[44]

Java was not to be his, as it was ceded back to the Dutch as part of the universal settlement following the fall of Napoleon. Instead he was made a member of the Privy Council and sent to India as Governor of Madras. This time most of his children and his beloved wife Margaret sailed with him. It was in Madras that she died.[45]

Hugh Elliot returned to England in 1820. On his way home he was forced by weather to spend some time on the isolated Atlantic island of St. Helena, then the exile of the Emperor of the French. He refused to set eyes on Bonaparte, let alone dine with him, considering him "to have been the greatest enemy his country ever had, and a curse to Europe."[46]

Elliot died in December, 1830, at the age of seventy-eight. He was remembered by his friends, his granddaughter later wrote, for "the felicity of his talk—so sparkling and so spontaneous—for the grace of his manner" and "by his descendants . . . for the gifts of heart and mind which made him beloved by a large and devoted family."[47]

The British nation buried him in Westminster Abbey.[48]

Henry Cecil Hodge, named for his uncle the Marquess of Exeter, an orphan before he was ten, lived to inherit and manage his father's plantation on Mount Bellevue. An 1840 visitor to Tortola reported: "This evening a fire broke out on the plantation of a Mr. Hodge, on the opposite side of the bay from our village. It was on a mountain in full view of our residence. It burnt with great rapidity, until the whole field of cane was consumed. The father of this planter was executed many years before for the murder of one of his slaves.

"During this fire my friend mentioned to me that this plantation had often been on fire. The relation of the melancholy fate of the father, and the repeated afflictions of the son, cast me into a sad train of thought—as if the hand of God was seen even now scourging with fire the spot upon which these cruelties had been inflicted on the helpless slave."[49]

EPILOGUE

"Utterly Abolished"

Statutes of the United Kingdom of Great Britain and Ireland, 3 & 4 William IV (1833), chapter 73:

> " . . . be it therefore enacted by the King's most Excellent Majesty, by and with the Advice and Consent of the Lords Spiritual and Temporal, and Commons, in this present Parliament assembled, and by the Authority of the same . . . that from and after the First Day of August One thousand eight hundred and thirty–four Slavery shall be and is hereby utterly and for ever abolished and declared unlawful throughout the British Colonies, Plantations, and Possessions Abroad."

BIBLIOGRAPHICAL NOTE

Original and contemporary source materials relating to the early history of the British Virgin Islands are scant and widely scattered.

The principal sources utilized in the writing of this book include the manuscript and published records of the prosecution and trial of Arthur Hodge, Governor Elliot's dispatches to Lord Liverpool, preserved in the Colonial Office files in the Public Record Office in London and Elliot's private papers, including family correspondence and drafts of his official dispatches, now in the National Library of Scotland in Edinburgh. The Marquess of Exeter kindly provided a copy of the Hodge-Hoggins marriage contract and Hodge's will was located in the British Virgin Islands' Archives in Roadtown. The Hodge coinage of Tortola is discussed in a 1915 article in the American Journal of Numismatics. Much concerning the motivation of the participants in the Hodge prosecution is found in William Musgrave's letter of January 30, 1811 located in the Elliot papers.

The early history of the Virgin Islands has been reconstructed from the Calendar of State Papers, Colonial Series, America and West Indies. George Suckling's *An Historical Account of the Virgin Islands in the West Indies*, published in 1780, is based on the author's period of service in the islands as Chief Justice and gives a view of their society during Hodge's young manhood.

Clement Caines' rare *History of the General Council and General Assembly of the Leeward Islands*, published in the Caribbean in 1804, and the anonymous *Authentic History of the English West Indies*, which appeared in 1810, aid greatly in the perception of life in the Leeward Islands during the Hodge period, as does Thomas Woolrich's testimony in the *Evidence of Witnesses Presented to the Committee Investigat-*

ing the Slave Trade, published by the House of Commons in 1790. Elsa V. Goveia's *Slave Society in the British Leeward Islands at the End of the Eighteenth Century*, is an excellent modern work on this subject.

Olaudah Equiano's 1790 autobiography is a classic which provides a rare view of Eighteenth Century slavery by one who had been enslaved. The descriptions of the mistreatment of slaves collected in Chapter 5 are drawn principally from the *Authentic History*, the *West Indian Sketches*, published in 1816, and Bryan Edwards' classic *The History, Civil and Commercial, of the British West Indies*.

The history of the abolition of the slave trade has been well–reported in several modern works cited in the bibliography and particularly in Lowell Joseph Ragatz' *The Fall of the Planter Class in the British Caribbean, 1763-1833* and Roger Anstey's *The Atlantic Slave Trade and British Abolition 1760-1810*. The quotations from Lord Mansfield's opinions are from contemporary law reports.

Hugh Elliot's European career was recorded in his granddaughter's *Memoir* and in Edmund B. D'Auvergne's *Envoys Extraordinary*. His letters to his wife reveal an educated, concerned and honorable man, and a loving husband and father.

Belisario's description of the slave cargo of the *Venus* and the information concerning George Martin's family and his will were found in House of Commons reports in the series of British Parliamentary Papers published by the Irish University Press.

Several years following the abolition of slavery in the British West Indies several American writers published reports on the changed conditions in the Caribbean islands. The description of the fire on the Hodge estate is from one of these, James Smith's *The Winter of 1840 in St. Croix, With an Excursion to St. Thomas and Tortola*.

The quote from the aged Virgin Islander concerning the importance of the Hodge affair is in Hazel Ballance Eadie's *Lagooned in the Virgin Islands*, published in London in 1931.

Modern works of value in understanding the history of the Caribbean islands include Sir Alan Burns' *History of the British West Indies* and Isaac Dookhan's *A History of the British Virgin Islands 1672 to 1970*.

A more complete bibliography follows.

BIBLIOGRAPHY

Official Documents

Commissioners for Trade and Plantations, *Journal*

Historical Manuscripts Commission Reports, No. 59

House of Commons, *Papers Relating To The West Indies, Viz. Correspondence Between the Earl of Liverpool and Governor Elliot; In reference to the Trial and Execution of Arthur Hodge, for the Murder of A Negro Slave, Ordered to be printed, 26 June 1811, No. 254; Papers Relating to the Prosecution Against Edward Huggins, Sen. at Nevis, Ordered to be printed 1st July 1811.*

House of Lords, *Papers Relating to the Trial and Execution of Arthur Hodge at Tortola, Ordered to be printed 1st July 1811, No. 114.*

House of Commons, *Accounts and Papers, 1790, Evidence of Witnesses presented to the Committee investigating the slave trade.*

Laws of the Island of Antigua, London, 1805.

Public Record Office, Admiralty, folio 51, Log of H.M.S. Cygnet, 1811.

Public Record Office, Calendar of State Papers, Colonial Series, America and West Indies.

Public Record Office, Colonial Office Papers, folios 152, 239, 314.

Third Report of Commissioner on Civil and Criminal Justice in the West Indies, 1825.

Other Sources

Abraham, James Johnston, *Lettsom, His Life, Times, Friends and Descendants*, London, 1833.

Anstey, Roger, *The Atlantic Slave Trade and British Abolition 1760-1810*, Humanities Press, Atlantic Highlands, New Jersey, 1975.

Baker, E. C., *A Guide to Records In The Leeward Islands*, University of the West Indies, 1965.

(Bayley, F. W. N.), *Four Years Residence in the West Indies*, London, 1831.

Belisario, Abraham Mendes, *A Report of the Trial of Arthur Hodge, Esq.*, London, 1811; Middleton, Connecticut, 1812.

Blackburn, Robin, *The Overthrow of Colonial Slavery, 1776-1848*, London, 1988.

Buchan, John, *Lord Minto, A Memoir*, Thomas Nelson and Sons, Ltd., London.

Burns, Sir Alan, *History of the British West Indies, Second Edition*, London, 1965.

Butler, Ewan, *The Cecils*, 1964.

Caines, Clement, *History of the General Council and General Assembly of the Leeward Islands*, St. Christopher, 1804.

Coke, Thomas, *A History of the West Indies . . . With An Account Of The Missions*, London, 1811.

Craig, William D., *Coins of the World 1750-1850*, Milwaukee, 1966.

D'Auvergne, Edmund B., *Envoys Extraordinary*, London, 1937.

Davis, David Brion, *The Problem of Slavery in the Age of Revolution 1770-1823*, Ithaca and London, 1975.

Derry, John W., *Castlereagh*, St. Martin's Press, New York, 1976.

Dookhan, Isaac, *A History of the British Virgin Islands 1672 to 1970*, Caribbean Universities Press, 1975.

Dunn, Richard S., *Sugar and Slaves*, Chapel Hill, 1972.

Eadie, Hazel Ballance, *Lagooned In The Virgin Islands*, London, 1931.

Edwards, Bryan, *The History, Civil and Commercial, of the British West Indies, with a Continuation to the Present Time*, London, 1819.

Equiano, Olaudah, *The Life of Olaudah Equiano or Gustavus Vassa written by Himself*, London, 1790.

Elliot, Hugh, *Papers*, National Library of Scotland.

Elliot of Stobs, Lady Dora, *The Elliots: the Story of a Border Clan: A Genealogical History*, London, 1974.

Foster, Joseph, *Alumni Oronienses: The Members of the University of Oxford 1715-1886*, Oxford, 1888.

Goslinga, Cornelis Ch., *The Dutch In The Caribbean And On The Wild Coast 1580-1680*, Gainesville, 1971.

Goveia, Elsa V., *Slave Society in the British Leeward Islands at the End of the Eighteenth Century*, New Haven, 1965.

Goveia, Elsa V., *The West Indian slave laws of the 18th century*, Caribbean Universities Press, 1970.

Gurney, John Joseph, *Familiar Letters to Henry Clay of Kentucky - Describing a Winter in the West Indies*, New York, 1840.

Harvey, A. D., *Britain In The Early Nineteenth Century*, St. Martin's Press, New York, 1978.

Inglis-Jones, Elisabeth, *The Lord of Burghley*, Faber and Faber, London.

Jenkins, Charles F., *Tortola*, London, 1923.

Knox, John P., *A Historical Account of St. Thomas, W. I.*, New York, 1852.

Lawrence-Archer, J. H., *Monumental Inscriptions of the British West Indies*, London, 1875.

Lewisohn, Florence, *Tales of Tortola and the British Virgin Islands*, Hollywood, Florida, 1966.

McQueen, James, *The West India Colonies: The Calumnies and Misrepresentations Circulated Against Them Examined and Refuted*, London, 1824.

Menkman, W. R., *Tortola*, West Indische Gids, XX (1938) pp. 178-192.

Minto, Countess of, *A Memoir of the Right Honourable Hugh Elliot*, Edinburgh, 1868.

Morison, Samuel Eliot, editor and translator, *Journals and Other Documents on the Life and Voyages of Christopher Columbus*, New York, 1963.

Murray, D. J., *The West Indies and the Development of Colonial Government 1801-1834*, Oxford 1965.

Oliver, Vere Langford, *History of the Island of Antigua*, London, 1896.

Pares, Richard, *War and Trade in the West Indies 1739-1763*, Oxford, 1936; Barnes & Noble, Inc., New York.

Pares, Richard, *A West-India Fortune*, London, 1960; Archon Books, 1968.

Penson, Lillian M., *The Colonial Agents of the British West Indies*, London, 1924.

Pitman, Frank Wesley, *The Development of the British West Indies*, New Haven, 1917.

Pope-Hennessy, James, *Sins of the Fathers*, London, 1967.

Porter, Dale H., *The Abolition of the Slave Trade In England, 1784 -1807*, Archon Books, 1970.

Ragatz, Lowell Joseph, *The Fall of the Planter Class in the British Caribbean, 1763-1833*, New York, 1928.

Rose, John Holland, *Life of William Pitt*, New York, 1824.

Russell, Jack, *Nelson and the Hamiltons*, London, 1969.

Sabine, Lorenzo, *Biographical Sketches of the Loyalists of the Revolution*, Boston, 1847.

Sherrard, Owen Aubrey, *Freedom From Fear*, New York, 1961; Greenwood Press, 1973.

Smith, James, *The Winter of 1840 In St. Croix, With An Excursion to St. Thomas & Tortola*, New York, 1840.

Southey, Thomas, *Chronological History of the West Indies*, London, 1776.

Stephen, James, *Reasons For Establishing A Registry of Slaves in the British Colonies*, London, 1815.

Stephen, James, *The Slavery of the British West India Colonies*

Delineated As It Exists Both in Law and Practice, London, Vol. I, 1824, Vol. II, 1830; Kraus Reprint, New York, 1969.

Stuart, Charles, *A Memoir of Granville Sharp*, New York, 1836.

Suckling, George, *An Historical Account of The Virgin Islands in the West Indies*, London, 1780.

Thomas, Hugh, *The Slave Trade—The Story of the Atlantic Slave Trade 1440–1870*, Simon and Schuster, 1997.

Truman, George, John Jackson and Thomas B. Longstreth, *Narrative of A Visit To The West Indies in 1840–1841*, Philadelphia, 1843.

Walvin, James, *England, Slaves and Freedom, 1776–1838*, University Press of Mississippi, Jackson and London, 1986.

Ward, J.R., *British West Indian Slavery, 1750–1834: The Process of Amelioration*, Clarendon Press, Oxford, 1988.

Watson, Richard, *A Defense of the Wesleyan Methodist Missions in the West Indies*, London, 1817.

(Wentworth, Trelawney), *The West India Sketch Book*, London, 1834, 1835.

Wesley, Charles H., *The Neglected Period of Emancipation in Great Britain 1807–1823*, Journal of Negro History, Volume 17, 1932.

Westergaard, Waldemar, *The Danish West Indies Under Company Rule*, New York, 1917.

Willert, P. F., *Mirabeau*, London, 1904.

Williams, Eric, *Capitalism & Slavery*, Chapel Hill, 1944; *History of the People of Trinidad and Tobago*, Port–of–Spain, 1962.

African Institution, *Reports of Directors, 1812–1815*.

American Journal of Numismatics, *The Coinage of the West Indies*, 1915.

The Annual Register For The Year 1811, London, 1812.

Antidote To "The West Indian Sketches" Drawn From Authentic Sources, No. IV, London, 1816.

Anti-Slavery Monthly Reporter, December 1826, May 1827.

Authentic History of the English West Indies, London, 1810.

Caribbeana, July 1914.

Christian Observer, No. 115, July 1811.

Edinburgh Review, November 1811.

Gentleman's Magazine, July 1811; *"Hugh Elliot: The Soldier–Diplomatist"*, 1901.

The Globe, London, 1811.

A Guide To Historic Places in the British Virgin Islands, B.V.I. Hotel and Tourist Association, 1979.

Howell's State Trials.

Laffi's Reports.

Legacy of the American Revolution to the British West Indies and Bahamas, Ohio State University, 1913.

Letters From The Virgin Islands, London, 1843.

Methodist Magazine, 1805.

Spink and Son, Numismatic Circular, June 1959, July–August 1959, July–August 1962.

A Review of the Reasons Given For Establishing a Registry of Slaves in the British Colonies, London, 1815.

Review Of The Quarterly Review; Or, An Exposure Of The Erroneous Opinions Promulgated In That Work On the Subject Of Colonial Slavery, London, 1824.

Shropshire Archaeological and Natural History Society Transactions, Series 4, Volumes 3 and 4, 1913, 1914.

The Slave Colonies of Great Britain or A Picture of Negro Slavery drawn by the Colonists themselves; being an Abstract Of the Various Papers Recently Laid Before Parliament On That Subject, London, 1825.

The Times, London, 1811.

West-Indian Sketches, Drawn From Authentic Sources, London, 1816.

NOTES

Notes to Introduction

1. *The Trial of Arthur Hodge, Esq. (Late One of the Members of His Majesty's Council for the Virgin Islands,) at the Island of Tortola . . . for the Murder of His Negro Man Slave Named Prosper*, stenographically taken by A. M. Belisario, Esq., (London, 1811; Middletown, Connecticut, 1812) [hereinafter cited as "*Trial*"], at pages 42 through 47 (page references are to the Middletown edition).

2. *Trial*, at page 77.

Notes to Chapter 1

The Settlement of the Virgin Islands: "Good Night Governor"

1. John Joseph Gurney, *Familiar Letters to Henry Clay of Kentucky —Describing a Winter in the West Indies* (New York, 1840) [hereinafter cited as "*Gurney*"], at pages 25, 28.

2. Governor Hugh Elliot to the Earl of Bathurst, Secretary of State for the Colonies, November 14, 1812, enclosing Virgin Islands census returns, Colonial Office Papers, Public Record Office, London [hereinafter cited as "C.O."] 152/100.

3. See, generally, Sir Alan Burns, *History of the British West Indies,*

Revised Edition (George Allen and Unwin, Ltd., London, 1965) [hereinafter cited as "*Burns*"]; Isaac Dookhan, *A History of the British Virgin Islands 1672 to 1970* (Caribbean Universities Press, 1975).

4.Andres Bernaldez, *Account of the Second Voyage of Christopher Columbus*; Samuel Eliot Morison, *Journals and Other Documents on the Life and Voyages of Christopher Columbus* (New York, 1963).

5.W. R. Menkman, "Tortola," West Indische Gids, Vol. XX, pages 178 to 192 (1938).

6.Calendar of State Papers, Colonial Series, America and West Indies [hereinafter cited as "*C.S P.*"], 1672.

7.*Id.*, 1675-1677.

8.*Id.*, 1720.

9.*Id.*, 1734.

10.*Id.*, 1735, No. 60.

11.John L. Anderson, *Night of the Silent Drums—A Narrative of Slave Rebellion in the Virgin Islands* (Charles Scribner's Sons, New York, 1975).

12.*C.S.P.*, 1735, No. 60.

13.*Ibid.*

14.*Ibid.*

15.Charles F. Jenkins, *Tortola* (London, 1923) [hereinafter cited as "*Jenkins*"]; James Johnston Abraham, *Lettsom, His Life, Times, Friends and Descendants* (London, 1933) [hereinafter cited as "*Abraham*"].

16.See, generally, George Suckling, *An Historical Account of The Virgin Islands in the West Indies* (London, 1780) [hereinafter cited as "Suckling"].

17.*Ibid.*

18.*Ibid.*

19.*Id.*, at pages 65 through 67.

20.Elsa V. Goviea, *Slave Society in the British Leeward Islands at the End of the Eighteenth Century* (Yale University Press, 1965) [hereinafter cited as "Goveia"], at page 63; C.O. 152/63.

21.Lorenzo Sabine, *Biographical Sketches of the Loyalists of the Revolution* (Boston, 1847) [hereinafter cited as "Sabine"]; *Legacy of the American Revolution to the British West Indies and Bahamas* (Ohio State University Press, 1913; reprinted with a new introduction and preface by George Athan Billias, 1972), at page 48.

22.Goveia, at pages 103-104; Lowell Joseph Ragatz, *The Fall of the Planter Class in the British Caribbean 1763-1833* (American Historical Society, 1928; reprinted, Octagon Books, New York, 1963, 1971) [hereinafter cited as "Ragatz"], at page 129.

23.C.O. 162/63; quoted in Goveia, at page 103.

Notes to Chapter 2

The Planters: "Sons of Indolence"

1.C.O. 152/100.

2.[Anonymous], *Letters from the Virgin Islands* (London, 1843) [hereinafter cited as "Letters"], page 211. Although not published until 1843, these letters were written during the reign of George IV, that is, in the 1820s (see page 76).

3.[Anonymous], *Authentic History of the English West Indies* (London, 1810) [hereinafter cited as "Authentic History"].

5.*Id.*, at page 65.

6.Letters, at page 53.

9.*Ibid.*

11.*Id.*, at page 8.

13.*Id.*, at pages 7-8. Suckling, at pages 7-8.

14.Authentic History, at page 9.

15.Clement Caines, *The History of the General Council and General Assembly of the Leeward Islands* (St. Christopher, 1804) [hereinafter cited as "Caines"].

16.Caines, at page 99.

17.*Id.*, at pages 97-98.

18.*Id.*, at page 83.

19.*Id.*, at pages 199-201.

20.*Id.*, at page 199.

21. Gurney, at page 28.

22. Authentic History, at page 46.

23. Caines, at page 180.

24. *Id.*, at pages 179-181.

25. *Id.*, at pages 189-190.

26. Authentic History, at page 8.

27. *Ibid.*

28. *Id.*, at page 10.

29. *Id.*, at pages 10-11.

30. Caines, at page 177.

31. *Id.*, at page 178.

32. Authentic History, at page 46.

33. *Ibid.*

34. Letters, at page 52.

35. Caines, at page 177.

36. Authentic History, at page 7.

37. *Id.*, at page 66.

38. *Id.*, at pages 7-8.

39. "I consider a woman who brings a child every two years as more profitable than the best man of the farm, what she produces is an addition to the capital, while his labors disappear in mere consumption.. . ." Jefferson to John Eppes, June 30, 1820 (Massachusetts Historical Society); quoted in Fawn M. Brodie, *Thomas Jefferson—An Intimate History* (W. W. Norton & Company, Inc., 1974), Chapter XXX at note 33.

40. Authentic History, at page 24.

41. Extracts of Minutes of Committee on the Slave Trade, House of Commons, 1790, testimony of Thomas Woolrich, [hereinafter cited as "Woolrich"], at page 110.

42. *Id.*, at pages 110-111.

43. Authentic History, at page 78.

Notes to Chapter 3

The Slaves: Africa and the Middle Passage:
"We Were Not To Be Eaten"

1. C.O. 152/100.

2. "Blacks are the same as other men; equal in every thing, except their wretched states, to the unjust and arrogant whites, who first degraded and now calumniate them." Caines, at page 124.

3. *Further Papers Relating to Captured Negroes*, ordered to be printed by the House of Commons, 16 March 1825 (Irish University Press, British Parliamentary Papers, Slave Trade, Vol. 67) [hereinafter cited as "Captured Negroes"], Separate Report of John Dougan, Esq., at pages 38-39.

4. Trial, at page 46.

5. Woolrich, at page 111.

6. *Ibid.*

7. Authentic History, at pages 24-25. See, generally, Bryan Edwards, *The History, Civil and Commercial, of the British West Indies (Fifth Edition, London, 1819)* [hereinafter cited as "Edwards"], Book IV, Chapter III.

8. *Id.*, at page 72.

9. *Id.*, at page 74.

10. *Id.*, at page 89.

11. Letters, at pages 200-205.

12. Edwards, at Book IV, pages 81-82.

13. Franklin W. Knight, *The Caribbean—The Genesis of the Fragmented Nationalism (Second Edition)* (New York, Oxford University Press, 1990), at page 173; Roger Antsey, *The Atlantic Slave Trade and British Abolition 1760-1810* (Humanities Press, Inc., Atlantic Highlands, New Jersey, 1975), at pages 38-39; David Brion Davis, *The Problem of Slavery in the Age of Revolution 1770—1823* (Cornell University Press, 1975), at page 57; Philip D. Curtin, *The Atlantic Slave Trade: A Census* (Madison, 1969). On

the slave trade generally, see James Pope-Hennessy, *Sins of the Fathers - A Study of the Atlantic Slave Traders (1441-1807)* (London, 1967) [hereinafter cited as "Pope-Hennessy"].

14. *Captured Negroes in the West Indian Islands, Apprenticed, Etc., 1811-1819*, ordered to be printed by the House of Commons, pages 84-88, reprinted in Irish Universities Press, *British Parliamentary Papers Relating to the Slave Trade*, Vol. 64, pages 92-96.

15. Olaudah Equiano, *The Life of Olaudah Equiano or Gustavus Vassa written by Himself* (London, 1790) [hereinafter cited as "Equiano," with page citations to the reprint of the autobiography published in *Great Slave Narratives* (selected and introduced by Arna Bontemps; Beacon Press, Boston, 1969)].

16. Equiano, at pages 27-33.

17. Id. at pages 32-33.

18. Authentic History, at page 25.

19. Equiano, at page 33.

20. Authentic History, at page 26.

21. Woolrich, at page 110.

Notes to Chapter 4

The Slaves: Life in the West Indies:
"A Predominant Melancholy"

1. *An Act for the good Government of Negroes and other Slaves, for preventing the Harbourage and Encouragement to runaway Slaves, and for restraining and punishing all Persons who shall abet the pernicious practices of trafficking with Slaves for any of the Staples, or other Commodities of these Islands, etc., etc., etc.*. [hereinafter cited as "Slave Act"], C.O. 152/67; see, generally, E. V. Goviea, *The West Indian Slave Laws of the 18th Century* (Caribbean Universities Press, Chapters in Caribbean History, 1970).

2. Slave Act, Clause 1st.

3. *Id.*, Clause 2nd.
4. *Ibid.*
5. *Id.*, Clause 3rd.
6. *Id.*, Clause 4th.
7. *Id.*, Clause 33rd.
8. *Id.*, Clause 9th.
9. *Id.*, Clause 6th.
10. *Id.*, Clause 8th.
11. *Ibid.*
12. *Id.*, Clause 15th.
13. *Ibid.*
14. *Id.*, Clause 24th.
15. *Id.*, Clause 27th.
16. *Id.*, Clause 18th.
17. *Id.*, Clause 43rd.
18. *Ibid.*
19. *Id.*, Clause 19th.
20. *Id.*, Clause 18th.
21. *Id.*, Clause 20th.
22. *Id.*, Clause 44th.
23. *Ibid.*
24. *Id.*, Clause 42nd.
25. *Id.*, Clause 23rd.
26. *Id.*, Clause 22nd.
27. *Id.*, Clause 45th.
28. *Id.*, Clause 29th.
29. *Ibid.*
30. *Id.*, Clause 30th.
31. *Ibid.*
32. *Ibid.*
33. Trial, at page 91.
34. Slave Act, Clause 31st.
35. *Id.*, Clause 39th.
36. *Id.*, Clauses 1st and 39th.
37. *Id.*, Clause 40th.

38.*Id.*, Clause 32nd.

39.*Ibid.*

40.Woolrich, at page 109; Caines, at pages 192 and following; Authentic History, at page 11.

41."Nothing displays the pride of the West Indians more than the number of slaves by whom they are attended.. . ." Authentic History, at page 11; Caines, at page 185; Letters, at page 52.

42.Authentic History, at page 11.

43.Authentic History, at page 24.

44.Caines, at page 209; Woolrich, at page 109.

45.Woolrich, at pages 108-109; Authentic History, at page 26.

46.Woolrich, at pages 108-109.

47.Caines, at page 166. "In all the islands, so far as he has seen, it is usual to turn the field negroes out to their work as soon as the light well appears, and they are not discharged from their drivers or overseers until the close of the evening, or dark." Woolrich, at page 108.

48.Woolrich, at page 105.

49.Caines, at page 167.

50.*Id.*, at page 168; Letters, at page 64.

51.Authentic History, at page 23.

52.Caines, at pages 160-165; Woolrich, at pages 108, 114.

53.Caines, at page 164.

54.*Id.*, at page 166.

55.Authentic History, at pages 63-64.

56.*Id.*, at page 24.

57.Woolrich, at page 105; Caines, at page 157.

58.Caines, at pages 156-157, 241.

59.Woolrich, at page 115.

60.*Id.*, at page 104.

61.*Id.*, at page 106.

62.Caines, at page 96.

63.*Id.*, at page 169.

64.*Ibid.*

66.Woolrich, at page 106.

67.Caines, at page 216.

68.*Id.*, at page 231.

69.Woolrich, at page 106.

70.*Ibid.*

71.Authentic History, at page 47.

72.*Ibid.*

73.Edwards, at Book IV, page 97; Letters, at page 150.

74.Letters, at pages 150-151.

75.*Ibid.*

76.Edwards, at Book IV, page 98.

77.*Ibid.*

78.Authentic History, at pages 64, 72.

79.Caines, at page 165.

80.Authentic History, at page 64.

81.*Ibid.*

82.Caines, at page 214.

83.*Id.*, at page 217.

84.*Id.*, at page 215.

85.*Ibid.*

86.*Id.*, at page 222.

87.*Id.*, at page 223.

88.Caines, at pages 224-229; Journal of the General Council of the Leeward Islands, March 27, 1798, page 36 (C.O. 152/78).

89.Caines, at page 225.

90.*Id.*, at pages 225-226.

91.*Id.*, at pages 227-229.

92.Caines, at page 229.

93.*Id.*, at pages 230-233.

94.*Id.*, at pages 233-234.

95.*Id.*, at page 235.

96.*Id.*, at page 237.

97.*Id.*, at pages 237-238.

98.*Id.*, at page 238.

99.*Id.*, at page 243.

100.*Id.*, at page 165.

101.Woolrich, at page 111.

102.Slave Act, Clause 43rd; Woolrich, at page 105.

103.Authentic History, at page 75.

104.*Id.*, at page 74.

105.*Id.*, at pages 75-76.

106.Edwards, at Book IV, page 102.

107.Authentic History, at page 75.

108.*Ibid.*

109.Edwards, at Book IV, pages 102-103; Authentic History, at page 75.

110.Caines, at pages 110-111.

111.Edwards, at Book IV, page 103.

112.*Ibid.*

113.Authentic History, at page 74.

114.Edwards, at Book IV, page 103.

115.*Ibid.*

116.Coke, at Vol. III, page 141.

117.*Id.*, at Vol. III, page 110.

118.Woolrich, at page 110.

119. Edwards, at Book IV, pages 70-72; Caines, at page 129.

120.Equiano, at page 12.

121.*Ibid.*

125.*Id.*, at Book IV, page 109.

127.*Id.*, at Book IV, pages 114-117.

128.Caines, at page 133.

130.Coke, at Vol. III, pages 141-142.

131.*Id.*, at Vol. III, page 142.

132.Edwards, at Book IV, page 104.

133.Authentic History, at page 64.

134.*Id.*, at page 11.

135.Edwards, at Book IV, pages 103-104.

136.Authentic History, at page 6.

137.Edwards, at Book IV, page 100.

138.*Id.*, at Book IV, page 114.

139.Letters, at page 148.

140.Coke, at pages 110-111.

141.*Id.*, at page 119.

142.*Id.*, at page 114.

143.Richard Watson, *A Defence of the Wesleyan Methodist Missions in the West Indies* (London, 1817) [hereinafter cited as "Watson"], at pages 119-120.

144.Jenkins, Chapters IV and V; Coke, at pages 125, 134.

145.*Id.*, at page 124.

146.Watson, at page 77.

147.Coke, at pages 125, 126.

148.For instances of the removal of Creole (native) slaves from Tortola to St. John and Trinidad during the 1820s see, "The Case of Miss Threlfall and Her Slaves," Anti-Slavery Monthly Reporter, No. 24, May 1827, at pages 384 (St. John) and 388 (Trinidad).

149.Watson, at page 118.

150.*Id.*, at page 70.

151.Caines, at page 131.

152.Watson, at page 73.

153.Caines, at page 131.

154.*Id.*, at pages 131, 132.

155.Edwards, at Book IV, page 85.

Notes to Chapter 5

The Slaves: Death in the West Indies:
"Mutilated Limbs and Broken Hearts"

1.Authentic History, at page 79.

2.Caines, at page 68.

3.*Id.*, at page 66.

4.Woolrich, at page 110.

5.Edwards, at Book IV, pages 83-84.

6.Richard S. Dunn, *Sugar and Slaves - The Rise of the Planter*

Class in the English West Indies, 1624-1713 (University of North Carolina Press, 1972), [hereinafter cited as "Dunn"], at page 324; Pope-Hennessy, at page 78.

7.Edwards, at Book IV, page 84.

8.C.O. 152/97; draft in Hugh Elliot Papers, National Library of Scotland, Edinburgh [hereinafter cited as "Elliot Papers"].

9.Caines, at pages 72-74.

10.Woolrich, at page 107.

11.Authentic History, at page 65.

12.Caines, at page 76.

13.Authentic History, at pages 6, 27.

14.Caines, at page 75.

15.Equiano, at page 76.

16.Authentic History, at page 80.

17.*Id.*, at page 65.

18.*Id.*, at page 79.

19. Slave Act, Clause 4th.

20.Governor John Hart to the Council of Trade and Plantations, *C.S.P.*, 1724, No. 260.viii, page 156.

21.Authentic History, at page 78.

22.Woolrich, at page 107.

23.*Ibid.*

24.*Ibid.*

25.*Id.*, at pages 107-108.

26.Authentic History, at page 79.

27.Woolrich, at page 109.

28.Slave revolts or conspiracies had occurred in Jamaica in 1655, 1690, 1694, 1754, 1760, 1765, 1769 and 1776 (Burns, at pages 335-336, 380-381, 383, 493, 496, and 511). See, also, Edwards, at Book IV, pages 74-79.

29.Burns, at pages 560-567.

30.Governor John Hart of the Leeward Islands, writing of Crab Island, which is located between St. Thomas and Puerto Rico, wrote, in 1724, that "I am apprehensive it would be impracticable to settle the same because the negroes would continually fly to the

Spaniards for refuge, who give them their liberty in one year after they are baptis'd." *C.S.P.*, 1724, No. 260.viii, page 156. See also, Journal of the Commissioners for Trade and Plantations, May 21, 1754 and February 25, 1765; C.O. 152/60, Burt to Germain, No. 93, September 26, 1780, quoted in Goveia, at page 255.

31. Coke, at Vol. III, page 124.

32. John Coakley Lettsom, *Memoirs of Dr. John Fothergill,* quoted in Jenkins, at page 43.

33. C.O. 152/69.

34. *Ibid.*

35. *Ibid.*

36. Authentic History, at pages 80-81.

Notes to Chapter 6

The Abolition of the Slave Trade: "It's So Odious"

1. Burns, at pages 122-123.

2. *Id.*, at pages 116-122.

3. *Id.*, at page 123. But see, Charles Stuart, *A Memoir of Granville Sharp* (New York, 1836) [hereinafter cited as "Stuart"], at page 29, arguing that the charge that Las Casas had suggested the importation of African slaves into Spain's American colonies was an unproven calumny.

4. See, generally, Hugh Thomas, The Slave Trade: The Story of the Atlantic Slave Trade 1440-1870; Pope-Hennessy; Reginald Coupland, *The British Anti-Slavery Movement, Second Edition,* (London, 1964) [hereinafter cited as "Coupland"]; Dale H. Porter, *The Abolition of the Slave Trade in England, 1784-1807* (Archon Books, 1970) [hereinafter cited as "Porter"].

5. Burns, at page 556.

6.See, generally, David Brion Davis, *The Problem of Slavery in the Age of Revolution 1770-1823* (Cornell University Press, Ithaca and London, 1975), Chapter 5, "The Quaker Ethic and Antislavery International."

7.Ragatz, at page 240; Coupland, at page 42.

8.*Ibid.*

9.*Ibid.*

10.Ragatz, at page 240.

11.Pope–Hennessy, at page 250.

12.Jenkins, at pages 53, 75, 79; *Captured Negroes*, at pages 118–124; James M'Queen, *The West India Colonies; The Calumnies and Misrepresentations Circulated Against Them Examined and Refuted* (London, 1824), at pages 169-173; George Truman, John Jackson and Thomas B. Longstreth, *Narrative of A Visit To The West Indies in 1840-1841* (Philadelphia, 1843), at pages 35-40, including the letter of advice written by Samuel and Mary Nottingham to their former slaves upon their emancipation.

13.See, generally, James Walvin, *England, Slaves and Freedom, 1776-1838* (University Press of Mississippi, Jackson and London, 1986).

14.Somerset v. Stewart, 20 Howell's State Trials 79, Lafft's Reports 1 (King's Bench 1772) [page citations herein are to Lafft's Reports], at pages 10, 15.

15.Ragatz, at page 244.

16.Stuart; Ragatz, at pages 244–246.

17.Ragatz, at page 245.

18.*Id.*, at pages 245-246.

19.*Id.*, at page 246.

20.20 Howell's State Trials 79, Lafft's Reports 1 (K.B. 1772).

21.60 U.S. (19 How.) 393 (1857).

22.347 U.S. 483 (1954).

23.Lafft's Reports, at page 2.

24. "In *England*, where freedom is the grand object of the laws, and dispensed to the meanest individual, shall the laws of an infant colony, *Virginia*, or of a barbarous nation, *Africa*, prevail?

From the submission of the negro to the laws of *England*, he is liable to all their penalties, and consequently has a right to their protection." Hargrave's argument on behalf of Somerset, Lafft's Reports, at page 5.

25.*Id.*, at page 17.

26.*Id.*, at page 18.

27.*Id.*, at page 19.

28.Ragatz, at page 247.

29.Stuart, at pages 29-31; Thomas Clarkson, *History of the Abolition of the Slave Trade* [hereinafter cited as "Clarkson", Vol. I, pages 95-97.

30.Stuart, at page 30.

31.Clarkson, at Vol. I, page 97.

32.Ragatz, at page 248.

33.*Ibid.*

34.*Ibid.*

35.Pope-Hennessy, at page 252.

36.Ragatz, at page 250.

37.Robert and Samuel Wilberforce, *The Life of William Wilberforce* (London, 1838) [hereinafter cited as "Wilberforce"].

38.Pope-Hennessy, at pages 264–272.

39. Wilberforce, at Volume I, pages 150–151.

40. Anstey, at page 267.

41.Ragatz, at page 251; Anstey, at pages 30–31, 269–270.

42.*Id.*, at page 252; Anstey, pages 271–272.

43.*Ibid.*

44.*Id.*, at page 253.

45.*Id.*, at pages 252-253.

2Robert E. Luster, *"The Amelioration of the Slaves in the British Empire, 1790–1833"*, American University Studies, Series IX (History), Vol. 134 (Peter Long Publishers, Inc., New York, 1995).

46.Goveia, at pages 33–34.

47.Caines, at pages 46–55; Journals of the General Council and General Assembly of the Leeward Islands, C.O. 152/78.

48.Journal of the General Council of the Leeward Islands,

March 1, 1798, pages 2–3 and Journal of the General Assembly of the Leeward Islands, March 1, 1798, pages 2–3, C.O. 152/78.

49.The Laws of the Island of Antigua (London, 1805), Vol. I, page 20 [hereinafter cited as "Melioration Act"].

50.*Id.*, Article I.

51.*Id.*, Article VI.

52.*Id.*, Article X.

53.*Id.*, Article X.

54.*Id.*, Article VII.

55.*Id.*, Articles XIX, XXVI-XXXIV.

56.*Id.*, Article XXII.

57.*Id.*, Article XLIX.

58.*Id.*, Article LI.

59.Porter, at page 120.

60.*Coupland*, at pages 152–153.

61.Porter, at pages 126-129; Ragatz, at page 276; Goveia, at page 39; Coupland, at page 106.

62.Porter, at pages 129–130; Coupland, at page 107; Goveia, at page 39.

63.C.O. 324/120-1; Porter, at pages 130–132; John Holland Rose, *Life of William Pitt* (New York, 1924), at page 503.

64.Anstey, at pages 264–376; Porter, at pages 133–134; Goveia, at page 40.

65. Anstey, at pages 375–376.

66.Anstey, at pages 391–396; Coupland, at page 109; Goveia, at page 41.

67.Porter, at pages 133–134.

68. Anstey, at pages 305–306, 373.

69. Anstey, at page 396.

70. Anstey, at page 397.

71.*Ibid.*; Anstey, at page 399; Coupland, at pages 109–110; Ragatz, at page 276; Goveia, at pages 41-43.

72.*Ibid.*

Notes to Chapter 7

Arthur Hodge:
"Great Accomplishments and Elegant Manners"

1.Caribbeana, Vol. III (1914) [hereinafter cited as "Caribbeana"], at page 302.

2.*Id.*, at pages 301-302.

3.*Id.*, at pages 301-303.

4.See, Ragatz, at page 22.

5.Joseph Foster, Alumni Oronienses: The Members of the University of Oxford, 1715–1886, Vol. II, at page 670 (London, 1888).

6.Public Record Office, War Office 255/116, Folio 63; Biographies of Officers 1689–1914, Regimental Museum of the Royal Welch Fusiliers; communication from the Regimental Museum to author, 19 December 1997; Hugh Elliot to Margaret Elliot, Tortola, May 9, 1811, Elliot Papers.

7.*The Times* (London), July 9, 1811, at page 4.

8.C.O. 152/69.

9.C.O. 152/70.

10.See, State of the Council of the Virgin Islands on the twenty fourth day of January 1811, C. O. 152/97.

11.Shropshire Archaeological and Natural History Society Transactions, Series 4, Volume 3, 1913 [hereinafter cited as "Shropshire Transactions"], at page 356; Will of Arthur Hodge, made December 1, 1810, Archives of the Virgin Islands, Roadtown, Tortola [hereinafter cited as "Will."]

12.Letter of Mr. W. Hutchinson, December 6, 1790, C.O. 152/70.

13.Watson, at pages 119-120.

14.Letters, at pages 274-275.

15.Trial, at page 24. In Hodge's will Peggy is described as "Negro" and Bella as "Mulatto." They were to be manumitted whenever the wife of his friend Dr. William West, to whom they were bequeathed, should leave the West Indies.

16.Indenture of Settlement dated 20/21 May 1800, located in the Exeter (Burghley) Papers, No. 69/46 [extract provided by the Marquess of Exeter].

17.*Ibid.*

18.Caribbeana, at pages 304–305.

19.J. H. Lawrence–Archer, Monumental Inscriptions of the British West Indies (London, 1875), at page 412; Dictionary of National Biography.

20.Caribbeana, at pages 302-305.

21.Goveia, at page 87.

22.Vere Langford Oliver, History of the Island of Antigua (London, 1896), [hereinafter cited as "Oliver"], at Vol. II, page 176.

23.See, generally, Elisabeth Inglis–Jones, *The Lord of Burghley* (Faber and Faber, London); Ewan Butler, *The Cecils* (London, 1964); Ravenscroft Dennis, *The House of Cecil* (Houghton Mifflin, 1914).

24.Salopian Journal, 11 June 1800 (quoted in Shropshire Transactions, at page 388).

25.Shropshire Transactions, at page 356.

26.Trial, at page 135.

27.Trial, at page 156 (testimony of Robert Green).

28.*Ibid.*

29.See, Plan of the British Virgin Island of Tortola, 1790, drawn by Robert Wilkinson [original in the British Library, London].

30.Authentic History, at pages 9-10.

31.C.O. 152/85.

32.The Act is reprinted in Spink and Son, The Numismatic Circular, July–August 1959 (London), at page 140.

33."The Coinage of the West Indies," The American Journal of Numismatics (1915), at page 95; F. Pridmore, "Notes on Colonial Coins. The Virgin Islands–Tortola-2," The Numismatic Circular (Spink and Son, London) July–August 1959, at pages 139–140. See, also, F. Pridmore, "Notes on Colonial Coins. The Virgin

Islands–Tortola," The Numismatic Circular, June 1959, and F. Pridmore, "Notes on Colonial Coins. A Sequel. The disposal of the Tortola Cut Money, 1892," The Numismatic Circular, July–August 1962.

34. Hugh Elliot to the Earl of Liverpool, Dispatch No. 42, May 15, 1811, C.O. 152/97.

35. Watson, at pages 79–80; Coke, at pages 126–131.

36. Watson, at page 80.

Notes to Chapter 8

Death on Mount Bellevue:
"That Modern Golgotha"

1. Trial, at page 16 (deposition of Stephen McKeough); Trial, at page 115 (testimony of Stephen McKeough).

2. *Id.*, at page 116 (testimony of Stephen McKeough).

3. *Id.*, at page 150 (testimony of George Davis Dix).

4. Trial, at page 25 (deposition of Stephen McKeough).

5. Trial, at page 8 (deposition of Perreen Georges); Trial, at pages 100, 104 (testimony of Perreen Georges).

6. Melioration Act, Article XIII.

7. Deposition of Stephen McKeough, March 15, 1811, in House of Commons, Papers Relating to the West Indies, No. 254; Correspondence Between the Earl of Liverpool and Governor Elliot in reference to the Trial and Execution of Arthur Hodge, for the Murder of a Negro Slave, ordered to be printed 26 June 1811 [hereinafter cited as "House of Commons"], at page 9, and House of Lords, Papers Relating to the Trial and Execution of Arthur Hodge at Tortola, Ordered to be printed 1st July 1811 [hereinafter cited as "House of Lords"], at page 11; Trial, at page 156 (testimony of Stephen McKeough).

8.House of Commons, at pages 8-9; House of Lords, at page 11 (deposition of Stephen McKeough).

9.Trial, at pages 17-19 (deposition of Stephen McKeough).

10.Trial, at pages 23-24 (deposition of Stephen McKeough).

11.*Ibid.*

12.Trial, at pages 11-12 (deposition of Perreen Georges). (The child's name appears as "Tamson" in House of Commons and House of Lords.)

13.Shropshire Transactions, at page 356.

14.Trial, at page 139 (testimony of Thomas Crook).

15.Trial, at pages 19,20 (deposition of Stephen McKeough).

16.Trial, at pages 20-21 (deposition of Stephen McKeough).

17.Trial, at pages 8-9 (deposition of Perreen Georges).

18.Trial, at page 10 (deposition of Perreen Georges); Trial, at page 23 (deposition of Stephen McKeough).

19. *The Living Lincoln*, Paul M. Angle and Earl Schenck Miers, editors (Rutgers University Press, 1955; Barnes & Noble, New York, 1992) at pages 66-68.

20. A. D. Harvey, *Britain in the Early Nineteenth Century* (New York, 1978) at pages 258-260.

21. James Stephen, *The Slavery of the West India Colonies Delineated*, (London, Vol. I, 1824, Vol. II, 1830; Kraus Reprint, New York 1969) [hereinafter cited as "Stephen"] at page 114.

22."But, unluckily for Hodge, he had been cruel to white as well as black men, and, being a noted duelist, was held in some dread by those against whom he conceived a spite." *Edinburgh Review*, November 1811, at page 143.

"He might have gone down to his grave with as much peace as his conscience would allow him, had he not, among his many demerits, been a notorious duelist," Edwards, at Book IV, page 459.

"I have read, and heard it asserted on the spot, that Hodge's ignominious death is, after all, attributable only to his unenviable notoriety as a duelist. . ..", Letters, at page 68.

"Mr. Hodge was celebrated as a duelist, and was said to have killed several men in duels," *West–Indian Sketches, Drawn From*

Authentic Sources, No. IV: The Nature of West-Indian Slavery Further Illustrated By Certain Occurrences in the Island of Tortola (London, 1816) [hereinafter cited as "West-Indian Sketches"], at page 34.

23. ". . . [A]nd I did appeal on my knees to the Almighty, to hear the prayer of the widow and orphan, and let him [Hodge] have his deserts, if it was even with hemp," (Trial, at page 152, testimony of Frances Pasea Robertson); "The finger of God has pointed out the son of this lady, to be with his divine aid, the avenger of her wrongs," (Trial, at page 176, closing statement of Solicitor General Paul Horsford, referring to William Cox Robertson).

24. Trial, at page 20 (deposition of Stephen McKeough).

25. Hodge's pride in his dueling pistols clearly appears in his will, preserved in the Archives of the British Virgin Islands, in which he specifically bequeathed a brace of pistols to each of two close friends.

26. Stephen, at page 117.

27. *Ibid*.

28. Id., at pages 116-117.

29. Trial, at page 20 (deposition of Stephen McKeough); page 154 (testimony of John Hanley).

30. Trial, at page 68 (opening statement of Henry Maurice Lisle for the Crown).

31. Trial, at pages 10-11 (deposition of Perreen Georges; pages 19-20 (deposition of Stephen McKeough); at pages 104-107, 109-110, 154-155 (testimony of Perreen Georges); pages 141-143 (testimony of Ann Arrindell); page 144 (testimony of Anne Rawbone).

32. Trial, at page 22 (deposition of Stephen McKeough).

33. *Ibid*.

34. Trial, at pages 25-26 (deposition of Stephen McKeough).

35. House of Commons, at page 9; House of Lords, at page 11 (deposition of Stephen McKeough).

36. Trial, at page 21 (deposition of Stephen McKeough).

37. Trial, at page 24 (deposition of Stephen McKeough).

38. "[T]his deponent cannot now remember all the names of

the negroes who have died in consequence of the cruelties of the said Hodge, but knows the number to be great; and that sometimes three and four have thereby died in the course of a day and night." Trial, at page 25 (deposition of Stephen McKeough).

"[H]e has lived with Mr. Hodge, at different times, for about three years, during which time he is satisfied that the said Hodge lost sixty Negroes at least by the severity of his punishments." House of Commons, at page 9; House of Lords, at page 11 (deposition of Stephen McKeough).

"His victims have been numerous, some of them were even buried in their chains." Hugh Elliot to Margaret Elliot, May 9, 1811, Elliot Papers, National Library of Scotland.

. 39. Trial, at pages 9-10 (deposition of Perreen Georges); pages 95-104, 110 (testimony of Perreen Georges); pages 111-113 (testimony of Stephen McKeough); pages 1201-121 (testimony of Mark Dyer French).

40. Shropshire Transactions, at page 356.

34. Trial, at page 131 (deposition of Penelope Hodge).

35. Christian Observer No. 115, July 1811; Review of Fifth Report of Directors of the African Institution, at page 443; West Indian Sketches, No. IV, at page 33.

36. Trial, at page 131 (deposition of Penelope Hodge).

37. Trial, at page 199 (testimony of Stephen McKeough).

38. Trial, at page 134 (testimony of Daniel Ross).

39. Trial, at pages 131-132 (deposition of Penelope Hodge).

40. Trial, at page 100 (testimony of Perreen Georges).

41. Trial, at page 151 (testimony of Frances Pasea Robertson).

42. *Ibid.*

43. Letters, at page 67.

44. Trial, at pages 111, 115 (testimony of Stephen McKeough).

45. Trial, at page 119 (testimony of Stephen McKeough).

46. House of Commons, at page 9; House of Lords, at page 11 (deposition of Stephen McKeough).

47. Will.

Notes to Chapter 9

Conflict and Accusation:
"Half–Uttered Threats"

1.Caribbeana, at pages 304-305.
2.Abraham, at page 455.
3.*Id.*, at pages 453-455.
4.*Id.*, at page 455.
5.William Musgrave to Hugh Elliot, Tortola, 30th January 1811, Elliot Papers, National Library of Scotland, Edinburgh [hereinafter cited as "Musgrave"].
6.*Ibid.*
7.*Ibid.*
8.*Ibid.*
9.Captured Negroes, at pages 38-39.
10.Musgrave.
11.The following account of events in Tortola in late 1810 and early 1811 is based, in large part, upon Musgrave.
12.A copy of the "Memorial, Remonstrance and Petition" of the House of Assembly is appended to Hugh Elliot to the Earl of Liverpool, Dispatch No. 38, 4th May 1811, C.O. 152/97.
13.Musgrave.
14.Will.
15.*Ibid.*
16.See Chapter 8, note 19.
17.Letters, at page 68.
18. Stephen, at page 117.

NOTES TO CHAPTER 10

The Governor:
"The Course of Duty"

1.For Elliot's life and career see, The Countess of Minto, A Memoir of the Right Honourable Hugh Elliot (Edinburgh, 1869) [hereinafter cited as "Countess"]; Hugh Elliot: The Soldier–Diplomatist, The Gentleman's Magazine, Vol. 290, pages 576-592 (1901); John Holland Rose, Life of William Pitt (New York, 1924); Edmund D. D'Auvergne, Envoys Extraordinary (London, 1937) [hereinafter cited as "D'Auvergne"].

2.The Annual Register, or a View of the History, Politics and Literature, For the Year 1811 (London, 1812), at page v; Dictionary of National Biography, entry on Sir Gilbert Elliot, First Earl of Minto.

3.The Complete Peerage (Doubleday and Howard de Walden, London, 1932), at page 713.

4.Porter, at pages 133-134.

5.D'Auvergne, at page 114.

6.Hugh Elliot to Col. C. W. Bigg, August 27, 1808, Elliot Papers, National Library of Scotland; Countess, at page 415.

7.He had been appointed Governor of Barbados in 1808, but did not assume the position. Robert H. Schomburgk, The History of Barbados (1848, reprinted by Augustus M. Kelley, New York, 1971), at pages 374-375.

8.Heydinger's letters to Elliot's children, preserved in the Elliot Papers in the National Library of Scotland, provide a refreshing counterpoint to Elliot's formal dispatches to the Colonial Office and his often troubled letters to his wife.

9.Elliot Papers.

10.Philip Heydinger to Harriet Elliot, Antigua, October 5, 1810, Elliot Papers.

11.*Ibid.*

12.*Ibid.*

13.Hugh Elliot to Margaret Elliot, Antigua, December 16, 1810, Elliot Papers.

14.*Ibid.*

15.Hugh Elliot to Margaret Elliot, Antigua, August 24, 1810, Elliot Papers.

16.Hugh Elliot to Margaret Elliot, St. Kitts, April 17, 1811, Elliot Papers.

17.Documents relating to the Huggins case are to be found in "Papers Relating to the Prosecution Against Edward Huggins, Sen. at Nevis, Ordered to be printed 1st July 1811," by the House of Commons [hereinafter cited as "Huggins Papers"] and in C. O. 152/96 and 152/97; see, Richard Pares, A West-India Fortune (London, 1950; reprinted, Archon Books, 1968), at pages 150-158.

18.Hugh Elliot to the Earl of Liverpool, Antigua, November 21, 1810, Huggins Papers, at page 14.

19.J. W. Tobin to Hugh Elliot, Nevis, September 7, 1810, enclosure to Hugh Elliot to the Earl of Liverpool, Antigua, November 20, 1810, Huggins Papers, at page 12.

20.Melioration Act, Articles IX and X.

21.J. W. Tobin to Hugh Elliot, Nevis, September 7, 1810, Huggins Papers, at page 11.

22.J. W. Tobin to Hugh Elliot, Nevis, September 7, 1810, enclosure to Hugh Elliot to the Earl of Liverpool, Antigua, November 20, 1810, Huggins Papers, at page 11.

23.Hugh Elliot to the Earl of Liverpool, Dispatch No. 27, St. Christophers, 21st February 1811, C.O. 152/97.

24.C.O. 152/97.

25.House of Commons, at pages 1-2; House of Lords, at pages 3-4.

NOTES TO CHAPTER 11

Hodge Arrested and Defended:
"Than To Kill His Dog"

1. Edwards, at Book IV, pages 459-460.
2. William Musgrave to Hugh Elliot, Tortola, April 2, 1811, enclosure to Hugh Elliot to the Earl of Liverpool, St. Christopher's, 16th April 1811, printed in House of Commons, at pages 11-13; House of Lords, at pages 13-15.
3. Trial, at page 7.
4. Trial, at pages 128-132.
5. Trial, at pages 8-12.
6. Trial, at page 58 (jury panel examination of Abraham H. Long); page 111 (examination of Stephen McKeough); William Musgrave to Hugh Elliot, Tortola, April 2, 1811, printed in House of Commons, at page 12 and House of Lords, at page 14.
7. Trial, at pages 12-14.
8. *Id.*, at pages 14-16.
9. *Id.*, at pages 130-132.
10. *Id.*, at pages 55-56 (jury panel examination of Robert Green).
11. *Id.*, at pages 16-28.
12. House of Commons, at pages 8-9; House of Lords, at pages 10-11.
13. Trial, at pages 120-121 (testimony of Mark Dyer French).
14. "I an instructed to say, the bones said to be Prosper's are now in court, and that some gentlemen went for the purpose of having them taken up." Trial, at page 125 (opening statement of George Tyson for the defense). "His victims have been numerous, some of them were even buried in their chains, and there have been found upon the bones taken from the graves chains & iron rings of near 40 Pounds weight." Hugh Elliot to Margaret Elliot, Tortola, May 9, 1811, Elliot Papers, National Library of Scotland.

"In these regions black evidence is not admitted, but in the present case, the opened grave of a murdered Negro discovered the skeleton, enveloped in chains of forty pounds weight, with which the unfortunate victim had been buried; and these bones, so manacled, were ready to be produced in Court by the Counsel for the Crown, had they proceeded upon subsequent Indictments." Hugh Elliot to the Earl of Liverpool, Dispatch No. 44, Tortola, May 18, 1811; C.O. 152/97.

15. Trial, at pages 28-30.

16. Trial, at pages 126-127 (opening statement of George Tyson for the defense).

17. Trial, at pages 32-34.

18. Trial, at page 77 (opening statement of Henry Maurice Lisle for the Crown).

19. House of Commons, at page 2; House of Lords, at page 4.

20. *Ibid.*

21. *Id.*, at pages 1-2; pages 3-4.

22. *Id.*, at pages 9-10; pages 11-12.

23. Hugh Elliot to the Earl of Liverpool, Dispatch No. 34, Antigua, April 1, 1811, C.O. 152/97; in House of Commons, at pages 1-2; House of Lords, at pages 3-4; original draft in Elliot Papers, MS 13055, f. 90v.

24. Hugh Elliot to the Earl of Liverpool, Dispatch No. 36, St. Christopher's, 16th April 1811, with enclosure, William Musgrave to Hugh Elliot, Tortola, April 2, 1811, C.O. 152/97; House of Commons, at pages 10-13; House of Lords, at pages 12-15.

25. Trial, at page 52.

26. Hugh Elliot to the Earl of Liverpool, Dispatch No. 35, St. Christopher's, 5th April 1811 C.O. 152/97; House of Commons, at page 10; House of Lords, at page 12.

27. Philip Heydinger to Harriet Elliot, St. Christopher's, April 17, 1811, Elliot Papers.

28. Hugh Elliot to Margaret Elliot, St. Christopher's, April 17, 1811, Elliot Papers.

NOTES TO CHAPTER 12

Trial:
"This Case—For the Honour of the World—Has No Parallel"

1. Trial, at page 172 (closing statement of Paul Horsford for the Crown).

2. Hugh Elliot to the Earl of Liverpool, Dispatch No. 37, Tortola, 3d May 1811, C.O. 152/97; House of Commons, at page 13; House of Lords, at page 15.

3. Trial, at page 60.

4. Log Book of *H.M.S. Cygnet* [hereinafter cited as "Cygnet"], Public Record Office (London), Admiralty Papers, Adm. 51/2037.

5. Hugh Elliot to the Earl of Liverpool, Dispatch No. 44, Tortola, May 18, 1811, C.O. 152/97.

6. See, Hugh Elliot to the Council and Assembly of the Virgin Islands, Tortola, May 10, 1811, enclosure to Hugh Elliot to the Earl of Liverpool, Dispatch No. 45, Tortola, May 18, 1811, C.O. 152/97.

7. Philip Heydinger to Harriet Elliot, St. Kitts, 14th April, 1811, Elliot Papers.

8. Philip Heydinger to Harriet Elliot, Tortola, 26th April 1811, Elliot Papers.

9. Cygnet.

10. Record of Trial, enclosure to Hugh Elliot to the Earl of Liverpool, Dispatch No. 37, Tortola, 3 May 1811, C.O. 152/97.

11. Trial, at page 186.

12. Trial, at pages 49-53.

13. Cygnet.

14. The account of the selection of the jury which follows is based upon Trial, at pages 54-61.

15. This statement would gain notoriety in subsequent com-

mentary upon the trial. See, The Edinburgh Review, November 1811, at page 144; West-Indian Sketches, at page 39.

16. Trial, at pages 62-121.

17. Trial, at pages 122-150.

18. Trial, at pages 150-157.

19. Trial, at pages 157-184.

20. "The Trial took place upon the 29th, and lasted from 10 o'clock in the Morning till Half past 5 o'clock in the Morning of the 30th." Hugh Elliot to the Earl of Liverpool, Dispatch No. 37, Tortola, 3 May 1811, C. O. 152/97.

"The Trial came on yesterday Morning at Ten o'clock, and lasted until half past five this Morning, when the Jury retired." Philip Heydinger to Harriet Elliot, Tortola, April 30, 1811, Elliot Papers.

21. Record of Trial, enclosure to Hugh Elliot to the Earl of Liverpool, Dispatch No. 37, Tortola, 3 May 1811, C. O. 152/97.

22. *Ibid.*

23. *Ibid.*

24. *Ibid.*

25. Trial, at page 185.

NOTES TO CHAPTER 13

Execution and Reflection:
"The Awful Signal"

1. Hugh Elliot to Margaret Elliot, Tortola, May 9, 1811, Elliot Papers.

2. Hugh Elliot to the Earl of Liverpool, Dispatch No. 39, Tortola, 9 May 1811, C.O. 152/97; House of Commons, at page 14; House of Lords, at page 16.

3. Hugh Elliot to the Earl of Liverpool, Dispatch No. 42, Tortola, 15 May 1811, C.O. 152/97.

4. Hugh Elliot to Margaret Elliot, Tortola, May 9, 1811, Elliot Papers.

5.Hugh Elliot to the Earl of Liverpool, Dispatch No. 44, Tortola, 18 May 1811, C.O. 152/97.

6.Trial, at page 142 (testimony of Ann Arrindell).

7.Hugh Elliot to the Earl of Liverpool, Dispatch No. 44, Tortola, 18 May 1811, C.O. 152/97.

8.Trial, at page 185.

9.The Times, 9 July 1811, at page 4.

10.Trial, at pages 185-186.

11.The Times, 9 July 1811, at page 4.

12.Hugh Elliot to Margaret Elliot, Tortola, May 9, 1811, Elliot Papers.

13.Philip Heydinger to Harriet Elliot, Tortola, May 8, 1811 (addendum to letter of 26 April 1811), Elliot Papers.

14.Hugh Elliot to the Earl of Liverpool, Dispatch No. 39, Tortola, 9th May 1811, C.O. 152/97; House of Commons, at pages 14-15; House of Lords, 16-17.

15.*Ibid.*

16.Hugh Elliot to the Earl of Liverpool, Dispatches Nos. 42 (15 May 1811), 43 (17 May 1811), 44 (18 May 1811) and 45 (18 May 1811), C.O. 152/97.

17.Hugh Elliot to the Earl of Liverpool, Dispatch No. 43, Tortola, 17 May 1811, C.O. 152/97.

18.Hugh Elliot to the Earl of Liverpool, Dispatch No. 44, Tortola, 18 May 1811, C.O. 152/97.

19.*Ibid.*

NOTES TO CHAPTER 14

Impact on History:
"The Hand of God"

1.Ragatz, at pages 384-385; Charles H. Wesley, "The Neglected Period of Emancipation in Great Britain 1807-1823," Journal of Negro History, Vol. 17, [hereinafter cited as "Wesley"], at pages 156-179 (1932).

2.Eric Williams, History of the People of Trinidad and Tobago (Port–of–Spain, 1962) [hereinafter cited as "Williams"], at page 50;Burns, at pages 574, 579.

3.See, generally, Williams, at pages 66-74.

4.D. J. Murray, The West Indies and the Development of Colonial Government 1801-1834 (Clarendon Press, Oxford, 1965) [hereinafter cited as "Murray"], at pages 80-81.

5.*Ibid.*; Ragatz, at page 389.

6.Murray, at page 80.

7.Huggins Papers.

8.The Earl of Liverpool to Hugh Elliot, Downing Street (London),27 January 1812, Elliot Papers.

9.The Globe (London), June 15, 1811.

10.Papers Relating to the West Indies; viz. Correspondence Between the Earl of Liverpool and Governor Elliot; In reference to the Trial and Execution of Arthur Hodge, for the Murder of a Negro Slave; Ordered, by The House of Commons, to be printed, 26th June 1811.

11.Papers Relating to the Trial and Execution of Arthur Hodge at Tortola; ordered to be printed 1st July 1811.

12.Christian Observer, No. 115, July 1811, at pages 440-445.

13.The Gentleman's Magazine, July 1811, at pages 79-80.

14.The Earl of Liverpool to Hugh Elliot, Downing Street (London), 20th June 1811; House of Commons, at pages 15-16; House of Lords, at pages 17-18.

15.A. M. Belisario to J. M. Belisario, Tortola, 6 August 1811, C.O. 152/98.

16.The Edinburgh Review, November 1811, at pages 129-149.

17.*Id.*, at page 139.

18.*Id.*, at page 149.

19.The Annual Register, or a View of the History, Politics and

Literature, For the Year 1811 (London, 1812), at pages 162-165.

20.Trial, at page 156.

21.Murray, at pages 93-95.

22.Ragatz, at page 390; Wesley, at page 168.

23.Murray, at page 95; Wesley, at pages 167-168.

24.Wesley, at page 168.

25.Murray, at page 97; Wesley, at page 171.

26.The Edinburgh Review, October 1815, at page 338.

27.West-Indian Sketches, Drawn From Authentic Sources, Nos. I through VIII (London, 1816-1817).

28.Antidote to "West-Indian Sketches" Drawn From Authentic Sources, Nos. I through IV (London, 1816).

29.Ragatz, at pages 398-399; Murray, at page 97.

30.See, *e.g.*, F. W. N. Bayley, Four Years Residence in the West Indies in the Years 1826, 1827, 1828, 1829 (London, 1831), at pages 384-392); James Smith, The Winter of 1840 in St. Croix, With An Excursion to St. Thomas & Tortola (New York, 1840) [hereinafter cited as "Smith"], at pages 82-83.

31.House of Commons Debates, March 16, 1824, at page 67; Stephen, Vol. I (1824), at pages 116–117.

32.[Trelawney Wentworth], The West India Sketch Book (London, 1834, Second Edition, 1835) [hereinafter cited as "Sketch Book"], at page 179.

33.Hazel Ballance Eadie, Lagooned in the Virgin Islands (London, 1931).

34.Hugh Elliot to the Earl of Liverpool, Dispatch No. 42, Tortola, 15 May 1811, C.O. 152/97.

35.Hugh Elliot to the Earl of Liverpool, Dispatch No. 38, Tortola, 4 May 1811, C.O. 152/97.

36.Hugh Elliot to _. H. Goulborn, (London), March 7, 1814, C.O. 152/104.

37.Oliver, at Vol. II, page 286.

38.Captured Negroes, at pages 38–39.

39.Sketch Book, at pages 199-202. Describing the judicial system in the Virgin Islands in the late 1820s, the author wrote,

"Justice, long reputed blind, had here all her other faculties impaired; and the moral dry–rot which was abroad, had been allowed to reach and to contaminate the very crutches on which she hobbled."

40. Sabine.

41. C.O. 152/104.

42. Mollie Gillen, Assassination of the Prime Minister (St. Martin's Press, New York, 1972).

43. The Earl of Bathurst to Hugh Elliot, Downing Street (London), June 22, 1813, Elliot Papers.

44. Hugh Elliot to the Earl of Bathurst, (London), February 11, 1814, C.O. 152/104; Murray, at pages 235–238.

45. Countess, at pages 411-413.

46. *Id.*, at pages 413-414.

47. *Id.*, at page 414.

48. *Ibid.*

49. Smith, at pages 82-83.

INDEX